YOU ARE MORE THAN YOUR JOB

MAKING A LIVING VS. MAKING A LIFE

EARL HARRISON

DEACONESS PRESS
MINNEAPOLIS, MINNESOTA

Published by Deaconess Press (a service of Fairview Riverside Medical Center, a division of Fairview Hospital and Healthcare Services), 2450 Riverside Avenue South, Minneapolis, MN 55454

Library of Congress Cataloging-in-Publication Data

Harrison, Earl.
You are more than your job : making a living vs. making a life / Earl Harrison.
p. cm.
Includes bibliographical references.
ISBN 0-925190-70-5 (pbk.) : $9.95
1. Work--Psychological aspects. 2. Identity (Psychology) 3. Conduct of life. 4. Self-esteem. I. Title.
BF481.H37 1993
158.7--dc20 93-6436
CIP

First printing: September, 1993

Printed in the United States of America

97 96 95 94 93 7 6 5 4 3 2 1

Cover and text design by Tabor Harlow

Publisher's Note: Deaconess Press publishes books and other materials related to the subjects of physical health, mental health, and chemical dependency. Its publications, including *You Are More Than Your Job*, do not necessarily reflect the philosophy of Fairview Hospital and Healthcare Services or their treatment programs.

CONTENTS

ACKNOWLEDGMENTS

First of all, I want to express my appreciation to the people I interviewed in connection with this book and whose stories make up such a significant part of it. For the sake of privacy, their actual names have been changed. What is unchanged is the integrity, creativity, and courage reflected in their stories. As I have read them many times, I have been repeatedly impressed by the quality of the lives of the individuals who shared themselves so generously. I sincerely thank each of them.

Let me also express thanks to Jack Caravela, Senior Editor at Deaconess Press, for his guidance, support, and patience in the process of bringing this book to completion.

In addition, I take this opportunity to acknowledge with gratitude the memory of my parents and the richness of their stories. And I want to thank my daughter, Lynn, and my son, Chris, for their interest in this project and, even more, for having contributed so much to my life.

Last but far from least, my deepest gratitude goes to my wife, Carol—for countless hours spent proofreading, for understanding and encouragement throughout this project, and, most of all, for her love and for the journey we have shared as husband and wife.

And so it is that this book is dedicated, with my love, to Carol.

INTRODUCTION

This book had its inception during a three-year venture of mine as owner of a personnel firm—otherwise known as an employment agency. That venture was part of an odyssey which had begun with my decision in 1978 to leave an academic position and which had led through consulting in connection with employee assistance programs to purchase of the personnel firm.

The purchase, I have to admit, was anything but a success. Like many people who go into business for themselves, I did so with less than adequate capital. By the time I closed the doors, my capital was less than it had been at the outset.

From the experience, however, I gained a new perspective—not only on unemployment, but on the relationship between paid work and how we tend to define ourselves. I suggest that not enough attention has been given to those matters.

The main thing that struck me was the fact that the meaning of employment goes far beyond money. A job does, of course, have to do with dollars and cents. But it also has to do with a sense of self-worth. It has emotional and spiritual implications as well as financial ones. Often, unfortunately, there is a shadow side to that truth—namely that people confuse who they are with what they get paid to do. They often define themselves almost exclusively in terms of what they do for a living. For those who are unemployed, therefore, the issue is not just loss of income; it is loss of perceived identity, loss of a primary way of defining themselves.

I had known those things on a different level before running a personnel firm. Having wended my way along a varied vocational path, part of which I outlined above, I sometimes had felt that I knew them all too well. But work in the personnel field added to my awareness. For I spent a large part of my time talking with unemployed people who came to my office, resumes in hand, as part of their search for jobs. They represented a cross section of the occupational spectrum. Many were very capable individuals with impressive work records. But what I began to realize, from their manner if not their words, was that in many cases their self-esteem was suffering as much if not more than their pocketbooks.

As I became increasingly aware of their plight, I began to search for resources which might be helpful to them. I found almost none. What I did find was that the most common approach to employment-related problems is to try to manipulate them along traditional lines. It consists of trying to create jobs through such things as government programs and tax incentives and of helping persons without work to develop strategies for reentering the work force. Consequently, there are numerous courses available for upgrading job skills and many books on how to write a resume, how to network, and how to handle interviews. For those who are employed but dissatisfied, there are books and courses to help them move up the career ladder. In short, the common approach to employment crises is to try to fix them simply by helping the individual to find another job.

We North Americans are quite good at fixing things—or at least at trying to fix them. It is a noble part of our history, part of our strength. And there is nothing fundamentally wrong with that kind of effort. It may be highly practical and beneficial. But the fact remains that the focus of much that is written about unemployment is on a solution that is external to the individual, something that is *out there.* And I know the limitations of that focus—from my own experiences as well as from those of people I have counseled.

For the external solution fails to deal with the need to find self-esteem and a sense of identity within rather than outside of oneself. To put it another way, the common approach to employment crises fails to address the questions that go beyond getting another job: *Who am I? What matters to me? What significance do I attach to what I do or want to do?*

We may think that such questions are only appropriate to persons in adolescence or young adulthood. But they are not limited to any stage of life. Even if we manage to sweep them under the rug, they inevitably resurface from time to time—especially those times when we feel most vulnerable. And we fail to honor them if we assume that they can be dealt with simply by putting things back together again—for example, by getting another job.

A related issue that tends to be skirted by most approaches to employment crises has to do with living in the present. Most approaches pay little attention to the matter of getting on with life while we wait—for another job, or a promotion, or whatever it is that we long for. But the present is where life is actually lived. And unless we learn to live as fully as possible in the present, in the here and now, we are only half alive.

These are the concerns which employment crises invite us to address. By and large, however, we fail even to be aware of that kind of invitation, much less to concern ourselves with it. This book will try to encourage you to respond creatively to the invitation and to the issues raised by it.

One reason we fail to address them is denial. There is a tendency on the part of many men, for example, to deny concerns about identity and self-esteem. The popular convention is that men are supposed to be strong, independent, and confident. They are supposed to know who they are. They are not supposed to experience self-doubt. Many men think that acknowledging such feelings is an admission of weakness, perhaps even a lack of manliness.

I'll be talking more about self-esteem throughout this book. For now, however, let me note that it isn't the same as bravado or egotism of excessive competitiveness. On the contrary, it is to be comfortable in your own skin. It is knowing that your worth derives not only from what you do but from who you are, not only from your paid work but from knowing and paying attention to your own values and priorities.

Healthy self-esteem is a blend of humility and confidence. It allows you to be at peace with yourself—not unaware of your limitations but not paralyzed by them. It fosters both personal growth and compassion toward others. It makes for less fear and more courage. It helps you to do your best and to be your best.

It would be a mistake, however, to believe that people with healthy self-esteem never feel discouraged, angry, sad, disgruntled, or out of sorts in any way. What is true, rather, is that there is within them a center of positive self-regard and acceptance which, while unavoidably affected by the ups and downs of life, provides a kind of ballast in the midst of them.

Our self-esteem is intertwined with our sense of self, with how we define ourselves. Both of these things, in turn, are related to every facet of our lives—including our employment. It is normal, therefore, that an employment crisis will pose a challenge to a person's self-esteem, no matter how healthy it is. But it does not have to be devastating.

Part of the way we handle that kind of challenge depends on what employment means to us. For it is one thing to see a job as an expression of self; it is another to see it as somehow conferring selfhood. It is one thing to find satisfaction in the workplace which is derived from a healthy sense of identity and self-esteem; it is another to *depend* upon a job for one's self-esteem, to *expect* identity to be conferred upon a person by virtue of his or her title, position, salary, or other work role amenities. Unfortunately, the latter assumption about the role of paid work is the operative one for many people.

Traditionally, women have tended to be defined in terms of their personal relationships. Traditionally, men have tended to be defined in terms of their relationship to their employment. In recent years, however, women have begun to define themselves more broadly. They have begun to move in greater numbers into fields previously dominated by men and in so doing they have lessened the kind of dependence on men that has traditionally been assumed and experienced. Which is as it should be. Unfortunately, however, greater emphasis on careers has led some women to fall into the same "self-as-job" trap that many men find themselves in.

Parallel to the development of new roles for women have been discoveries about the family dimension of addiction and alcoholism. In that context we have become aware of the perils of what has come to be termed "codependence" in personal relationships—which, understood broadly, means looking to someone else for one's identity and happiness.

I suggest that all of us, both men and women, now need to look at our relationship with paid work in the same kind of light. It is not that employment is bad—any more than caring for another person is bad. It is, rather, that a certain kind of relationship with paid work can be limiting—just as can be true of some relationships with other people. It is one thing to invest ourselves in our jobs; it is another to hope that our jobs will somehow invest us with an adequate sense of self.

I am not suggesting that employment is unimportant. On the contrary, employment meets many human needs—and not only monetary ones. It often plays a very significant role, for example, in ego development—which is vital to personal growth. It frequently has a social component, encouraging us to interact with other people. In addition, it provides a sense of security, a sense of place.

Nevertheless, we need to remember at least three things. One is that the role we play as breadwinner, as provider, is only *one* of the roles we play. Our roles will differ a bit from person to person, but we all have a variety of them. Part of dealing with employment challenges is learning to pay attention to those other roles, learning to value them, and learning to value ourselves through them. We need to honor the fact that there are things we do which do not involve pay but which are just as important and significant—perhaps even more so—than those we get paid to do.

The second thing we need to keep in mind is that work has a meaning that goes beyond employment. To cite but a few examples, we "work" on our golf game or our tennis game; we "work" on our relationships; people speak of "working" a recovery program. And the list could go on. The point is that our work goes beyond the "bottom line." It can involve both self-expression and self-discovery—whether on the job or elsewhere. We work at the things we care about. And, in the process, we work on ourselves.

In our culture, work that involves pay is deemed to be our "real" work. All other parts of our lives, we are led to believe, are secondary. But I want to suggest that our *real* work is the work we do on ourselves and on behalf of others. Work, in that sense, involves not only making a living but *making a life*. It has to do not only with the means of living, but with the *art of living*—and with the meaning we attach to all the things we do.

Work, in this sense, encompasses all of our parts—including our ability to play. It encompasses, moreover, a dimension of selfhood which is more than any of its external expressions, more than the sum total of all of its parts—a part of all of us which underlies all of our outward expressions.

That part of ourselves has been spoken of over the centuries—directly or indirectly—by poets, philosophers, and spiritual teachers from many traditions. It may be given different names: "soul," "spirit," "center," "essence," "true self," "authentic self," and the like. It is not susceptible to weighing and measuring but, if we let ourselves, we can come to know it.

One way of understanding this matter is to use the analogy of clothing. What we wear is a major part of who we are. But most of us have more than one outfit. We need to give ourselves permission to feel valuable in all of them—and, if we choose, to wear with pride those that are hand tailored as well as the ones which are ready made. And we need to remind ourselves that we are more than any clothes we wear. Marketing adages notwithstanding, clothes do not "make" the person.

Throughout this book, I will be making a distinction between paid work—employment or job work—and the work that involves our whole person, the inner man or woman as well as the outer one, our being as well as our doing. In some cases, to be sure, they overlap and complement each other. But our job work self needs to be the servant of our true self, not the other way around. And we need to remember that although inner work can and does go on in the framework of paid work, it can also continue apart from it.

Let me emphasize, however, that work in the comprehensive sense I am talking about here is not simply a navel-gazing enterprise. Working out our potential is never done fully in isolation. It takes our relationship with paid work and with other people seriously. Implicit in it is awareness of the truth that no one is an island unto himself or herself.

The final theme I want to identify in this book is that employment crises can open the way to a deeper, more satisfying, and more empowering sense of who we are. It is not simply that such crises can encourage us to do something different—they can open the door to a more complete way of being.

From what I have said, it should be clear that this book is not primarily about finding another job. There are many fine, readily available resources which address that challenge well. I recommend that you avail yourself of them as needed.

Nor is the book only intended for those who are unemployed or concerned with some other kind of immediate employment crisis. I hope, rather, that it can be of value to anyone at any stage of life, regardless of whether he or she is employed or unemployed.

This book is really an invitation—and a reminder. It is literally a "re-minder" that what we do or don't do in the workplace is not the same as who we are. And it is an invitation to find strength and value in parts of ourselves that we may have neglected, parts which we may be only dimly aware of if at all, parts which await being recovered—or discovered.

The operative words are "process" and "journey." For although most of us continue to seek a fixed identity—and are led to believe we should understand ourselves in that manner—the truth is that we are always in the process of becoming. We are always journeying. And thus we need to find ways of affirming ourselves along the way.

Most of the ideas in this book are not new. Many of them, in fact, are ancient. But they tend to be easily forgotten and they are not often applied to our relationship to work. They repeatedly need to be awakened in us; *we* repeatedly need to be awakened to *them*. We need, moreover, to focus on the ways in which they are relevant to issues having to do with selfhood, work, and employment.

Learning to see ourselves as more than our jobs is not easy. The notion that we are what we do may be less pronounced than it was a few years ago, but it is still the operative one for most people. It is a notion that is deeply imprinted in us—mentally, emotionally, and socially. Changing it represents a major transition, a kind of odyssey. As such, it requires both *unlearning* and *relearning*.

In the course of this book we will be offered help with these concerns by some people who have achieved a view of themselves which goes beyond the workplace. For some of them, the end result of this process was noticeably different from the one they expected at the starting point. In other cases, the change, though no less significant, was less obvious to outside observers. In some cases, unemployment was part of the story; in others, it was not. Particulars aside, all the people you will meet now know that they have many dimensions and that they are more than the paid work they do.

It is important to understand that the issues to be discussed in this book do not lend themselves to easy answers. The stories and ideas set forth here, moreover, are not intended to provide simple solutions or some kind of system or formula. And they are certainly not intended as a substitute for counseling, employment or otherwise. The ideas and stories presented here should be seen, rather, as suggested guidelines for a process which is, by its very nature, heuristic and open-ended, more cyclical than linear.

We seldom if ever grow mechanistically. Instead, we most often move by jumping ahead and doubling back. The person past middle age may, therefore, find himself or herself dealing with issues of adolescence when it comes to exploring their relationship with and understanding of work. Alternately, those in adolescence or young adulthood can have challenges thrust upon them which seem more appropriate to later stages of life.

As a result, the manner in which the ideas and insights presented here are selected, combined, and applied will vary greatly from individual to individual. The people who have shared their stories, moreover, can speak only for themselves. Their stories are intended, however, to stimulate your imagination and provide encouragement on the journey toward a sense of self which is based on more than paid work. But the journey itself—and the satisfaction which comes with it—will come about only if we are willing to make it for ourselves.

Chapter One

PROBING THE SELF-AS-JOB SYNDROME

"So what do you do?"

That question is part of the small-talk repertoire of just about everyone. It gets asked at cocktail parties, neighborhood gatherings, church socials, by the person next to us on the plane, train, or bus. What it means, of course, is: *"What do you do for a living? What job do you hold?"*

The question, as we all know, represents a kind of social shorthand. And as such, some might argue, it's really not very consequential. After all, they could say, we don't really want to know the details of what a person *does.* We just want a label, something to identify the person.

But the problem is that what is often communicated is the deeper question: *"Who are you?"* For rooted in our culture is what I am terming the "self-as-job syndrome"—the belief that selfhood is all but synonymous with employment or its equivalent

People who are employed and fairly comfortable in their jobs tend to have little or no problem with the question, *"What do you do?"* And the answer usually takes the form of an *I am* statement: *"I am a lawyer...an electronic technician...a carpenter;" "I am a hair stylist...a disc jockey...a housewife."* Or the person may be more specific: *"I am the regional sales manager of the bracket division of ABC Widget Company."* In some cases, to be sure, the answer is something like, *"I work for thus and such company."* But all too often the response begins with *"I am."*

The situation is quite different for those who are unemployed, underemployed, or retired, those who feel they are not being true to themselves in the work they are doing, or those whose employment cannot be neatly encapsulated in a simple sentence. When asked the question, *"What do you do?"* it is not unusual for people who fall into any of those categories to mumble something vague and, as quickly as possible, change the subject. Although they may not identify themselves in terms of a job, they reveal, by their manner if not their words, that they too consider paid work to be the operative framework for defining a person.

Most of the time, of course, we probably don't think much about this matter. As long as things are going along routinely it isn't an issue. But then we are confronted by a change, perhaps by a crisis. Unemployment is an increasingly common one. Retirement is another. In both cases people often become aware—sometimes very painfully—of how much they have defined themselves by their paid work.

Or we may be jolted by what is termed a "mid-life crisis." It may or may not be outwardly dramatic. But we wake up one day to find that our work-related image of ourselves as an "accomplisher" no longer feels as important as it once did. It may have all but disappeared, but we are not quite sure where, or what to do. We may feel that everything we have valued, including the way in which we defined ourselves, is gone or is rapidly slipping away.

In response to such crises—whether involving loss of employment or disillusionment with the work ethic or both—we may struggle in a multitude of ways to reclaim whatever it is we feel we have lost. If we have lost our job, we may expend all our time and energy trying to find a new one. If we're still employed, we may throw ourselves all the more intensively into the job we have. We may also try other tactics such as changing our spouse or lover, taking a vacation, drinking or eating too much, or engaging in promiscuous sex. In those and a myriad of other ways, we try to regain some semblance of control over life and to escape the feelings of vulnerability that seem to lurk everywhere.

This may seem like a men's issue, and to some extent that perception may be true. Men in our culture have tended more than women to define themselves primarily in terms of employment. In recent years, however, the situation has become more inclusive as society has changed its expectations of women. For example, writer Judith Viorst reported in her book *Necessary Losses* that in the mid-1970s most of the mid-life women she knew were planning to reenter the job market. And, while emphasizing that many reasons were given for wanting paid employment, she noted that the following kind of statement was common: "I have to have a job, or who will I say that I am when I go to a party?"*

In some cases, of course, a woman's desire for a sense of identity from a job may be part of the so-called "empty nest syndrome"—the loss felt by some women when their job as a mother is no longer so necessary. And a related fact is that motherhood no longer occupies quite the same role as it once did. Some young mothers are criticized by their peers for being "nothing but mothers." The corporate world evidently has little sympathy for females who opt for what is sometimes termed the "mommy track"—making motherhood a higher priority than a career.

Likewise, a young career woman I know admits that cutting back on her career to have a child will be something of a threat to her identity. And a female architect I interviewed, who was never inclined toward the life of a nun, told me that at one point her career was so consuming that for five years she had virtually no personal life—a fact that she realized only in retrospect and which has virtually excluded the possibility that she will ever have children.

Still, the rise of the career woman is relatively recent. Thus for many women the meaning of employment may be significantly different than what it is for men. It may, that is, be a way of getting to know themselves more fully—of discovering a way to be "more than" the roles traditionally assigned by society. For men, on the other hand, job work is almost invariably a way of sticking with an assigned role.

It seems to me, however, that there are at least two elements here which cut across gender lines. One is that in our culture the freedom to engage in paid work is often associated with healthy ego development in adults. (Nothing in this book is intended to deny the importance of that truth, or of the fact that needs associated with ego development may occur at any age or stage of life.) Nevertheless—and this is the second factor common to both sexes—neither men nor women have to be defined solely by the work they do for pay. They do not have to be defined in nothing but commercial terms.

There is a sense in which doing one's job—what we would term employment—has probably always provided a measure of personal satisfaction and self-esteem. It is not hard to imagine, for example, a primitive hunter feeling good about himself for having literally brought home the bacon. And the same would have been true of others in the clan, including the women, who probably not only prepared the food but fashioned the pots in which it was cooked.

In those scenarios, however, jobs were done in a framework quite different from the one that is operative for many if not most people today. For one thing, they involved a skill or a craft—hunting, fighting, weaving, tilling the soil, preparing food. There was therefore a strong element of personal creativity and satisfaction. One could see the results—and the benefits—of his or her work. Moreover, most work was motivated by basic human needs rather than by a desire to accumulate wealth. And, finally, tasks were done on behalf of a supportive, closely-knit community. The tribe or clan was like an extended family—at least far more so than are most modern workplaces.

The origins of the mindset toward work that is common to the majority of North Americans go back about three centuries—roughly to the time of the Protestant Reformation. It was a period marked by major changes not only in religion, but in economics and what we would term psychology and sociology. And one significant result, emphasized by social psychologist Eric Fromm, was the widespread belief that success at what I am terming "job work" was a sign of God's favor—a sign of being among the "elect"—and that failure at that type of work was a sign of damnation.* As a result, Fromm argues, people began to be driven to be productive "not so much by external pressure but by an internal compulsion..."* People began to work to "prove" something—to themselves and to others—rather than simply to provide for basic needs.

The potentially positive side of that development—which over a period of time became what we know as the Protestant Work Ethic—is that it encouraged the view that all of life is holy. It helped to break down artificial divisions between the sacred and the secular. Theoretically, at least, it was a reminder that there is more to work than financial reward.

Unfortunately, it also had an additional twist, namely that by the 18th Century and the time of the Industrial Revolution, work as personal fulfillment had come to be subordinated to work as productivity.* Job work had come to be seen as more important than work on behalf of the whole person. The self-as-job syndrome had come to be part of the established order.

One reason the new attitude toward work caught hold as well as it did was that it emerged around the same time as the modern notion of individualism. In England and western Europe class structures had begun to dissolve and social mobility was becoming more common. People started to be enamored with the idea of self-definition as opposed to being defined by the group or family into which one was born. And thus the middle class as we know it began to be visible.

Of perhaps even greater significance was the fact that these ideas—religious and secular—appeared just prior to the colonization of North America. Conditions were therefore ripe for them. For one does not have to be a historian to understand that a work ethic which stressed individualism and was motivated by concern for salvation would be very well suited for settling a new world. And it was not hard for the settlers to go one step further and conclude that commerce in general had the blessing of God.

The kind of drive spurred by that message has undoubtedly contributed greatly to what we view as productivity and accomplishment. But we have paid a price for our success. We have valued the material at the expense of the spiritual. We have paid attention to ego concerns while neglecting the needs of the inner person. In our emphasis on productivity, we have been indifferent to its effects on the earth and the atmosphere. *For all its benefits, the work ethic—which is really the success and accomplishment ethic—has had a significant downside.*

One part of that truth is that individuals ceased to have a natural, established place in the economic and social order.* The positive side of that development, of course, was the breakdown of a system in which people found it difficult if not impossible to move out of the class or strata into which they were born. But the negative effect was that a sense of connectedness and of self-definition in the framework of community began to be less important. What we sometimes call rugged individualism came to be the dominant motif and, with it, the widespread mandate to make some*thing* of oneself.

It is not surprising, therefore, that a side effect of our culture's blend of individualism and obsession with job work has been a heightened sense of loneliness. In response to that fact, people have searched—and continue to search—for security, for wholeness, for ways in which to meet human needs which in other times have been met by closely-knit communities. And there is nothing wrong with that kind of quest.

Unfortunately, however, we often settle for less than the real thing. Our focus becomes fixated—in some cases, exclusively—on the horizontal dimension of life rather than the vertical one. We pay more attention to external realities than to internal resources. We perpetuate another unfortunate part of our legacy, namely that personality is a commodity.* Our sense of "self" is often derived primarily from the image we present and the responses we get from other people.

That fact is reflected not only by what I am calling the self-as-job syndrome, but also by the fact that we often buy things as a way of trying to prove our worth. Which is hardly surprising, given that we are part of a culture in which consumerism has been carried to degrees never before known. We are constantly being urged to partake of a smorgasbord of options for instant gratification of desires we may not even have known we had. Competition plays a part in our consumption as well as in our production. Keeping up with our neighbors has become the rule rather than the exception for an increasing number of people. Conspicuous consumption is no longer limited to the very wealthy. And one argument—perhaps heard less than it was for awhile but still around—has it that whoever has the most "toys" when he or she dies is the "winner."

Those values, of course, are reflections of a larger kind of mindset which dominates our culture. We live out our lives in the context of what could be called "the mechanistic imagination." Although it may be changing a bit, the machine is still the western world's dominant model for humanity. Only that which can be weighed, measured, counted, taken apart and put back together again is thought to be "real."

Make no mistake about it: we have benefitted greatly from the scientific approach to life. Without it we would not be able to enjoy many things we take for granted—television, freedom from many diseases, and jet travel, to name only a few. Unfortunately, it lends itself to the shortsighted view that only that which is tangible really matters. And that viewpoint, in turn, helps to account for the fact that money—and what it can buy—is the virtually unquestioned unit for assessing value in our culture.

In his book, *Money and the Meaning of Life,* philosopher Jacob Needleman argues that money originally evolved as a means of maintaining a link between the spiritual and the material in human life.* But now it has become quite literally the "bottom line," the prism through which everything is viewed. It is almost impossible to think of anything with a value we take for granted which is not framed in monetary terms. It may be true that money will not buy everything. But it is also true that we tend to want—or to acknowledge wanting—"only the things that money *can* buy."*

If you doubt that money is the primary means by which we define value, consider the following. A person may be better at something he or she does not get paid for doing than for something which does involves income—growing roses, for example, as opposed to, say, selling shoes. Or one's volunteer work may be of greater personal consequence than one's job work—visiting shut-ins, for instance, versus routine clerical work. Even in the face of such contrasts, however, most people will likely see themselves as being defined by their paid activity. And that fact will probably be true even if the person hates whatever the paid job happens to be.

Which is not to question the importance of working for pay. It is simply to note the pervasiveness of a particular framework of values and to try to illustrate its flaws. For the truth is that payment doesn't always determine the importance of work, and that one can be productive with or without a paycheck.

The problems associated with the emphases and values I have been outlining have, of course, been exacerbated by the fact that we live in a period of time marked by mobility and mind-boggling change. In every arena—politics, science, religion, economics, sociology, education, sexual behavior, business—things simply are not "staying in place." Lifestyles, families, roles, and relationships—all have become much more diverse in recent years. And the changes go on.

Many of them have a bearing on job work and our relationship to it. Prior to World War II, for example, it could still be argued that employment was mainly a means of supporting a family, of providing for basic needs and a few comforts. And it still is for many people. In the boom period following the war, however, upward mobility became increasingly important. As a result, men—and in recent years, women—have begun to spend more time and energy on the career track. Indeed, they are *expected* to spend more time on it.

All of these changes, of course, affect the family unit and can aggravate whatever dysfunctionalism may be inherent there. I have no wish to elaborate on those issues. Suffice it to say that dysfunctionalism in families means that basic human needs do not get adequately met, especially in the formative years of development. Lack of inner confidence and low self-esteem often result from those circumstances, and, in turn, can make people prone to become obsessive about whatever offers security or the illusion of security—including job work.

At the same time, technology continues to develop apace and corporate culture continues to expand through takeovers, the growth of conglomerates, and the movement toward a global economy. In the process, individuals are engulfed—and, in many cases, dispensed with—while the notion that people are defined by their role in the workplace continues to be pervasive.

This cursory review is surely not intended to be a comprehensive explanation of all of the factors that contribute to commitment to hard work and the self-as-job syndrome. There are undoubtedly many I have not included here, including ones particular to cultures outside of western Europe and North America.

The intention, rather, is to increase our awareness of at least a few of the factors, historical and contemporary, which influence our particular view of ourselves and work. And given these factors, it seems to me all too understandable that people who are unemployed, underemployed, or retired can be devastated by the question *"What do you do?"* Nor is it surprising that others are often obsessively attached to their employment, clinging to it as if it were the sum total of their identity.

The point is that we are heirs of a viewpoint which emphasizes definition and identity by way of an external part of life rather than in terms of the inner person—a legacy which lends itself to obsessive commitment to work. Given that perspective, job work can provide a simple ready made solution which can be effectively applied to many problems—at least in the short term. It also means, however, that being without paid work can easily be felt as being without an identity.

Which seems to me to speak of the need for alternatives.For the prevailing viewpoint is just that—*a point of view.* It is not, however, the only one. As I will be suggesting throughout this book, there are other viable stances toward living and working. There is good reason to believe that human beings do not have to be defined solely in terms of the workplace—certainly not in terms of the kind of workplace that is so common today. There is good reason to believe that job work is not the only way in which we can be productive and find meaning. And there is good reason to believe that letting go of the self-as-job kind of identity, though difficult to do, can be freeing and empowering.

A number of people I interviewed knew all too well what it is like to be obsessively attached to their employment. One is a man I'll call Leon, an accounts manager for a company which became involved in several mergers in the late 1980s. It was a period of great stress for employees of the several companies involved, and Leon was no exception. The stress exacerbated a serious health problem he had lived with for years and in 1988 his position was declared redundant. It was a devastating experience for him.

"Work represented not only your livelihood but your manhood. That's the way I approached my job. I put it before everything else, my family and myself included. I put in more hours than was thought reasonable by a lot of people, and even if I had problems myself, they took second place to my job. I was brought up to believe that loyalty to the company was of utmost importance no matter what, and I operated on that basis. I became a company man no matter what I was working at or who I was working for."

He described his feelings about losing his job as "complete and utter devastation, absolutely. I was robbed of any self-esteem I had. My self-worth became absolutely nil. I thought very seriously, on more than one occasion, of doing away with myself."

Ralph, another man I interviewed, experienced a variation of the same story. Coming from an immigrant background which placed great emphasis on hard work, Ralph took that emphasis seriously and during the first few decades of his professional life he moved easily and successfully through several careers—including teaching and work as a seminar leader and business consultant. "I never had to look for a job," he recalled. "Even making the change from education to business was a smooth transition."

But then the onset of life-threatening medical problems brought to a halt the particular path he was on. And, faced with that reality, he was forced to take a fresh look at that path. "I had allowed it to consume me completely," he admitted. "I was spending virtually all my time at getting ahead. I was spending very little time with my family. I had come from a background where I had been very much involved in the community in various ways, and I had dropped all of that. I had not been to the church where I was a member for several years.

"I had a very large number of acquaintances, but I had no close friends. I was always away from home, and as a family or as a couple we had no friends because as one of a pair that is never there you don't fit in anymore.

"When the whole thing came crashing down, the first thing that hit me was what kind of dream I was chasing that eliminated so many of the things that traditionally had been of very great importance in my life. I came to the conclusion that it was an empty dream. It was a dream that could never give me the fulfillment I was looking for."

Yet another person who had a similar attachment to employment was Cheryl, the female architect I mentioned earlier. Although she spent several years travelling when she was in her 20s, Cheryl admitted to having "been very work oriented. I wanted something that would really grip me." That something turned out to be architecture, and a number of jobs she described as "incredibly exhilarating. I worked all the time. I would come in early and leave late." The first position was especially exciting. "I had an important job, my first job after getting my college degrees, so that was my identity. I knew that architects dropped like flies, but I was sure that I wasn't going to be one of those people."

As it turned out, she was one of those people—and not once but several times. And, after one layoff, she realized that "I had not had any physical intimacy in my life for five years, which was a big shock to me. I'd completely forgotten about it. When I discovered this fact I realized it was the whole five years I had been working as an architect." And, she recalled, "I was so driven by architecture that I forgot that I could have children." Now in her mid-40s, she admitted that she has "twinges" about not having become a parent. "But I realize that I made a choice—though coming to that understanding took many months of talking with my counselor and going over things and crying a lot and being very angry."

And this group would be incomplete without reference to a man I'll call Brian. Prior to losing his job, Brian had held senior administrative posts in a major university for more than twenty years. His reaction on learning of his job termination was quite succinct: "I thought to myself, `I don't think I'm going to be able to survive. My job is my identity. What am I going to say to my wife?'"

In the course of this book I will be talking more about Leon and Ralph and Cheryl and Brian—and others—all of whom have made significant and fulfilling changes in their lives. But I want to emphasize now that no judgment is intended concerning the choices made in these or other stories. It would be a mistake, for example, to infer from Cheryl's experience that sexual activity and bearing children should be more important to women than having a career. And it is both understandable and commendable that people approach a new career with commitment and enthusiasm.

The object, rather, is simply to take a second look at the kind of self-as-job identification which is the norm for many if not most people—and to remind ourselves that there are other options for defining selfhood and finding self-esteem.

We need to remind ourselves, moreover, that it is one thing to see employment as self-expression and something different to see it as a crutch essential to one's sense of self. It is one thing for job work to be an integral part of creative living. It is another for it to be an attachment motivated by fear for one's sense of identity.

One way to determine the significance you attach to your role in the workforce is to try to identify the most fearful thing—or things—about being without it. For some of you reading this, of course, being without a job requires no imagination. But what may require a bit of effort is discovering what it is about that situation that causes the most anxiety.

It is obvious, for example, that when we're without a job we will likely feel concern about paying the bills. But for most of us, the anxiety goes deeper. It is one thing to feel anxiety about not being able to meet basic human needs. It is another to have a vague sense that your very *being* is threatened, or to be anxious about being unable to maintain a standard of living which is intended to prove one's self-worth.

And a second kind of analysis you might consider has to do with whether you believe that fixing your employment problems would fix all of your other outstanding concerns. Granted, if you are without a job, getting one might enable you to alleviate the problems you are having with your creditors. And taking steps to find a job might well strengthen you within and in the process help you deal with other outstanding issues. But to see employment as having the potential to fix all of our concerns is to fail to be in touch with the deeper parts of ourselves.

However well we may understand these matters in theory, the fact remains that moving away from the self-as-job syndrome is a major transition. For one thing, doing so may mean giving up the kind of illusion spoken of by psychiatrist Roger Gould, who argues that the world of business—and, by implication, many parts of the larger world of job work—has "banned human frailty...and replaced it with the dictate that success can cover up any flaw."*

And perhaps the even greater part of the difficulty lies in the fact that letting go of *any* perceived identity is difficult. In fact, it may even be that we can become *addicted* to our identity, to our image of ourselves. That is the opinion of another psychiatrist, Gerald May, who argues that "representations of self habituate, adapt and control us," that we "may cling to them more tenaciously than to any other attachments" and that letting go of them "can indeed feel like death."*

But the truth is that some illusions have to be given up and that our pact with a fixed identity has to be broken—or at least modified—if we are to move to a deeper and ultimately more satisfying sense of who we are. As more and more of us are being challenged to let go of the self-as-job image of ourselves, we need to remember that truth. We need to remember that we have to let go to grow, that letting go invites us to make new discoveries about ourselves, other people, and the world in which we live. It offers us new ways of seeing ourselves and new options for living and working.

One way of trying to understand the meaning of job work is to identify some of its components. One is that employment provides us with a ready made sense of being valued, of being productive. We are exchanging our ability, time, and energy for money, and there is no doubting the appeal of that kind of exchange. But it is primarily to the ego. It is part of the viewpoint which would have us believe that the more money people make the more valuable they are. It is associated with intense concern about upward career mobility, achievement, and outer success.

Another value we may see in job work is that it allows us to provide not only for ourselves but for those about whom we care. Job work driven by that kind of motivation may or may not have much to do with one's ego. It may well be that the value attached to doing the job has to do not so much with pride or satisfaction as simply with the fact that it allows a person to pay the rent and to feed his or her children. The operative word is "provider."

A third potential appeal of job work is that it can provide personal satisfaction. It can be an act of self-expression, of creativity. It can allow a person to use skills and abilities which reflect her or his values and priorities. Payment may be involved, but what is really important is the satisfaction.

Earlier I spoke of the importance of job work vis-a-vis ego development. As I am using the word here, ego refers to a kind of container within our personality.* It therefore needs to be strong enough to hold and protect what we value. Job work can be enormously helpful in strengthening that container. It can help us to develop that part of our identity. Thus it is understandable that we feel an attachment to our job work and that we often derive great satisfaction from it.

But I also contend that we need to keep that matter in perspective. For the developmental journey, while it involves the ego, can also take us beyond it if we are willing. We journey to establish a social identity, yes. But that effort should be seen as part of a process, not as a fixed and final end result.

It is important, that is, not to become so attached to the container that we neglect to nourish what it contains. To do so is to shortchange ourselves. It is to fail to know the strength that comes from soul and spirit and the dimension of selfhood that goes beyond ego. And, paradoxically, a break in the container can be an opening to those deeper realities and resources.

Part of our North American idealism is that job work can satisfy all of our needs—for money, for security, for both personal and professional satisfaction. The important thing, we are told, is to know what we care about and then find a way to do it for pay. The argument is that people can find personal fulfillment and be productive and make money at the same time.

I surely do not want to question in any way the value of finding job work that is satisfying and lucrative. It is a worthwhile objective and one that should be pursued with all appropriate means. But the experience of most people is that circumstances are rarely that ideal. Certainly many people in and out of the workforce today—or at any time in history—would testify without hesitation to that fact. For in the job context the emphasis remains on the side of economic productivity, and that fact seems unlikely to change in the much-heralded "new world order." Even if we do what we love, moreover, and even if it brings us a bundle of money, it will still be the case that our true selfhood encompasses more than our job work.

Given that fact, it seems to me we need to be clear about our concerns and our options with respect to employment and the assorted crises so often associated with it. And so I come back to the fact that we use the word "work" in connection with many things having nothing to do with employment—including the games that we allegedly "play" during our "leisure" time.

That tendency, of course, can be seen as an example of the fact that many people do not know how to play very well. It can be seen as part of our Puritan heritage, which includes distrust of anything pleasurable. But it may also reflect the fact that there is something inherently pleasurable in work itself—at least when it pertains to mastery of a skill and/or personal growth.

To put it another way, we work at the things that we care about—on and off the job. Thus we may work harder at home over the weekend than we do in the office, factory, or store during the week. And we find satisfaction in that kind of work. We need to give ourselves permission to value the work that matters to us—whether or not it involves pay—and to value ourselves apart from any kind of work.

The fact is that for most people job work is valuable precisely because of what it pays. And in a way that fact is unfortunate. It seems to be a further indication that human beings are primarily commodities, that our worthiness has to do only with monetary concerns, only with the ubiquitous bottom line. But that assessment is true only if we choose to make it so.

On the other hand, that is, valuing job work for its monetary compensation can mean that we give employment its proper due but do not impose undue significance on it. Such a viewpoint is not inconsistent with some approaches to spirituality which, in effect, recommend that people have a means of making a living for the sake of being able to support their *real* work. One historical example that comes readily to mind is St. Paul, who often supported himself as a tentmaker.

The problem comes when people value themselves *only* in terms of what they earn and then make the jump from job self to total self. The result is that they see both the latter and the former in monetary terms. However understandable that fact may be, it is sad. For human beings are more than units of productivity and monetary value. (Employers, of course, will probably continue to view most employees in that way; it is unlikely that their viewpoint is going to change.) But people *can* choose alternate ways in which to view *themselves*. We do not have to limit ourselves to the world of job work in our quest for identity and meaning and self-esteem.

One potentially useful way of approaching the relationship between real work and job work is what a psychologist named Kathleen Riordon Speeth terms "making a living with your left foot." By that phrase (which is also the title of a workshop she has done on occasion at Esalen in California) she means that people should take their paid work seriously but that they should balance it with interests that are often more meaningful to them.

Of course, people do that kind of thing all the time—when they work at one or more meaningless jobs for the sake of providing for their children, for example. But the approach can also be understood in broader terms.

I am thinking specifically of struggling artists who routinely make a distinction between who they are and what they do for a living. They may wait on tables or do sales work for a living. But they see themselves as painters, poets, actresses, or musicians.

Their paid work is important, but they know their real work to be something else. Through their job work they provide for themselves what at various times in history has been provided by patrons of the arts.

That kind of stance is difficult to maintain—and probably more so today than in times past. There have been times, for example, when it was quite acceptable to be an amateur poet or painter or musician. Now, however, there is a tendency to regard creative activities as frivolous unless one is earning money from them, and to view with amusement or downright ridicule individuals who persevere in them. For instance, the waitress who declares "I'm really an actress" is a ready made target for cartoonists and comics.

It is true, of course, that the self-esteem and sense of identity of such persons may well be strengthened when and if they begin to receive payment for their talent. Depending on their commitment and mixture of ego and inner strength, however, they may manage to stay true to their priorities, even if their income is derived from jobs that have nothing to do with their real work.

One example that comes to mind is an artist I know of who, though having obvious talent, chose for many years to do his art while making his living in a different field. And I am also thinking of a friend of mine, a professional actor, who for many years has divided his time between acting and driving a taxi. I have heard him speak of his commitment to the craft of acting as having provided meaning and significance for him in the midst of a good deal of personal stress over the years.

I believe we can and should learn from such people. I know I draw strength from being reminded of them. For they offer us a better-than-usual understanding of what it means to have a true sense of identity and self-esteem. They take time or, probably more accurately, *make* time for what matters to them deeply.

We all have that option open to us. To fail to claim it is to fail to draw upon a resource which can contribute greatly to our sense of identity and self-esteem. To express what lies within us—whether through art, music, words, or in sundry other ways—is to tap into that part of us that is most authentic.

Which brings me back to the distinction between job work and what I am terming "real" work. Job work, to be sure, gets most of our attention. It is, after all, what we get paid to do—or what we do for those who are providing our livelihood. And largely because of the real importance of money we tend to think of job work as being our true work.

But the irony of the self-as-job syndrome is that we may identify with our paid work even while often hating it. We frequently dream of saying "take this job and shove it," but if that same job is *taken away,* we may feel bereft of what we perceive as our primary identity. We are often caught in a quandary—feeling that we can't live with our employment and that we can't live without it.

Which points up the truth that we need to take real work seriously—work concerned with personal growth and development and with the needs of other human beings. That work may or may not involve pay. It may well include *play.* It may give meaning to paid work, especially when that work is routine and mundane.

There may be times when work on ourselves and on behalf of others has to continue in spite of the absence of paid work. It may be that such work helps us to deal with the times when there is no paid work.

What constitutes real or true work will vary greatly from individual to individual. For some it may have to do with relationships. For some it will involve pursuit of activities we traditionally define as creative, such as writing, drawing, and music. Still others will see it in terms of community activity and social concerns. In some cases it may involve learning to be less serious, more playful. But whatever its configuration, we must pay attention to our real work if we are to know who we truly are.

What I am talking about here goes by a number of terms—self-realization, self-discovery, self-actualization. All of them are valuable. They point to the importance of developing all parts of ourselves, our wholeness. I will be using each of them in the course of this book.

But I want to emphasize again that I am not talking about a completely private process. The journey of self-discovery—which is a phrase I will be using often—has implications beyond the individual. Developing the inner life does not exclude involvement in the outer world. The two go hand in hand.

We need to remember, moreover, that almost any job can be part of our true work or can complement true work. But it is never all of it. Almost any job can also be a denial of real work—a way of avoiding it. The significance of paid work with respect to inner work will be determined in part by things such as one's responsibilities and one's stage in life.

But we also need to know that the work of self-development and self-actualization can happen at *any* stage of life and can continue regardless of our employment status. One of the themes of this book is that unemployment may be a call to delve more deeply into our real work—which includes our *being* as well as our *doing*, our play, our leisure, the questions we ask as well as the answers we find.

Employment provides us with affirmation (pay) for doing certain types of activity—those which will produce the end results which others desire. Part of the challenge is to find ways of affirming not only what we *do*—on the job and elsewhere—but who we *are*. In that framework not-doing may be as important as doing—or even more so. In the framework of true work—in contrast to job work—there may be times when "working" includes deliberately not working.

One job-related word that is valuable in talking about real work is the word "calling," which is sometimes used as a synonym for the word "vocation." Both are words we do not often hear anymore. Others, such as "career" and "profession," are a good deal more common. And yet, like many things which get neglected, the notion of calling offers a richness that we would do well to heed.

Traditionally, a call is thought of as having to do with a religious vocation—or, perhaps, a creative one. And both of those connotations still hold true. But underlying them is another truth, namely that having a vocation means being called to a particular task. And the deeper meaning of the task, whatever its particulars, has to do with responding to an inner urge to be one's true self with integrity and authenticity. To say yes to that kind of call is to have a vocation; it is to work at developing one's unique abilities and giftedness.

That approach to calling allows us to understand it as referring not only to specific activities but to the process of realizing our potential. It may encompass what a person does but more importantly it has to do with who a person is—and is becoming. It has to do with the question *who am I?* and with an answer that goes beyond any relationship to the marketplace. It should be understood in terms of purpose, meaning, reason for living, and an individual's relationship with the wider community.

In the course of the book I'll have more to say about the notion of calling. But for now, the important thing is that we understand the concept in broad rather than narrow terms and recognize that it can be a source of strength. It can provide a "why" for living even when the "how" is not immediately clear. It can provide us with an empowering way of viewing ourselves.

Deep down inside, all of us want to move toward fulfillment, toward realization of our potential. But our tendency—especially when life is going along smoothly—is to conclude prematurely that we have "arrived," that we have gotten to our destination before we really have. From that perspective, which reflects the dominant values of our culture, what we are paid to do or have been paid to do may seem like all there is to us.

It is easy to assume that there is nothing in us to be realized other than what can be measured in marketplace terms.In some cases, we deny that there is a dimension to life that goes beyond what we do in the marketplace. Or, if we do have inklings of a deeper dimension, we may convince ourselves that it can be fully realized through paid employment.

As a result, we confuse meeting spiritual needs with accumulating material success. We seek that which is good but go to the wrong address to find it. We become fixated on something which, while important to ego development, is only one part of true selfhood.

To be sure, our employment or its equivalent will almost invariably be a significant part of our self-realization. It may even be the single most important part of it—at least for a time in life. But it is not the whole. Which is why a time of employment transition may offer a unique opportunity to reclaim parts of ourselves that have previously been neglected. We can learn to view ourselves as valuable with or without a means of livelihood.

We tend to give ourselves credit for the things we do well which are in keeping with what we perceive as our assigned roles in life. Those roles may have to do with personal relationships; they may have to do with work relationships. In most cases, they are important. It is right that we should take them seriously.

But we also have the right to give ourselves credit for the things we do which are important to us but which may involve activities which go beyond what we think of as our assigned roles. In recent years women have begun to claim that right, particularly with respect to personal relationships. Now, it seems to me, both men and women should feel free to claim that sort of right as an alternative to being defined solely according to paid work.

The bottom line is that reframing our relationship with employment—and our relationship with ourselves when we are without employment—is part of the overall challenge confronting both men and women in today's changing world. And implicit in that challenge is the opportunity to move to a new and more empowering sense of self-worth.

There have been times in the past when that kind of opportunity could be ignored with seeming impunity. If a person lost or quit a job, he or she could probably get another one—perhaps quite soon. Often there was little time for deeper concerns to surface, much less to be acted upon.

Today, however, the situation is different—and is likely to remain so. Increasingly, people are being forced to confront the reality that job work is not everything. Layoffs and early retirement are becoming more and more common for people across the occupational spectrum. For many, finding new employment which is similar to that which has been lost is proving to be difficult if not impossible. Whatever the shape of the much-heralded new world order, it seems likely to present serious challenges to the sense of selfhood found in the workplace. Thus it is increasingly hard to ignore the fact that to define oneself exclusively in terms of employment is to shortchange oneself.

It is not that we should ignore job work. We can choose, however, to see it in a fresh perspective. We can choose to claim for ourselves priorities beyond the workplace—priorities which, if we are true to them, can help us to affirm and value ourselves as whole persons. We can choose to affirm ourselves, at least in part, by way of activities with significance that goes beyond a paycheck, even beyond measurable achievements.

We may, for example, find that doing something with one's children, spouse, lover, or friends is as important as doing the next deal. We may discover an unexpected source of strength and sense of identity by putting aside our own concerns for a time and turning our attention to the needs of those less fortunate than ourselves. We may decide that our own creativity deserves as much attention as the next rung of the career ladder.

At their best, both job work and play are vital parts of our real work. At its best, employment is a significant part of inner work. But it is also true that making a life is about more than making a living, that real work is more than job work, and that who we are is more than what we do. We discover those truths by making choices, by responding, by struggling, and by journeying. It's a process we have already begun. Let us now continue it.

Chapter Two

THE GOODBYE/HELLO PROCESS

One essential element in getting to know our beyond-the-workplace self is honoring the process involved, including the painful parts. In making that statement I am not recommending self-pity. On the contrary, the object is to avoid self-pity, to see viable alternatives to the victim stance. What I am urging is honesty over denial—which is the necessary starting point for any healing and growth. I am urging that we pay attention to feelings such as grief, shame, fear, anger, regret, failure and loneliness. For by doing so we learn about important parts of ourselves that are "more than" our surface identity.

That approach is contrary to much popular advice—which says "hurry up, get over it, fix it, get on with getting ahead." But to heed that advice is to fail to attend to parts of ourselves that need to be heard. It is to pretend that only the "positive" parts are real—much as a corporation going through upheaval might try to pretend that the concerns of anxious employees are not real.

Denial does not eliminate the legitimacy of concerns that get neglected; rather, it only adds to their intensity. Taking them seriously, on the other hand, can help us move toward greater health and strength. And so it is with feelings such as grief, anger, fear, shame, regret, and loneliness. They are the voices we try not to acknowledge in our routine, workaday existence, and thus they often do not get heard. But they are no less real and no less a part of one's total self. To ignore them is to do ourselves an injustice. It is to refuse to open ourselves to new levels of insight, creativity, and strength.

Of course, if unemployment is involved, there may well be some urgency about finding another job. And if so, it is important to deal with that matter as expeditiously and skillfully as possible. Many good books are available, and you may find it helpful to become acquainted with the strategies they recommend and to make use of them as appropriate.

But whatever priority we may give to finding another job, it is important to remember that our real work can go on in the process. We can use the experiences of making phone calls, sending out resumes, having interviews, and suffering rejections as a way of learning more about ourselves. We need to be aware of what is going on inside as well as outside of us during the process, and to see what we can learn from our reactions. Remember that we do not deal with personal development issues separate from the ones we may regard as more "practical." The latter are grist for the mill of the former.

No matter what the particulars, it is important that we make our way out of the uncomfortable space we are in by going through the process, painful as it may be, of dialoguing with parts of ourselves that we may have ignored and all but forgotten. We need to remember the truth contained in so many myths and spiritual traditions: the dragons have to be dealt with before it is possible to live happily ever after, and the desert has to be gone through before arriving at the "promised land."

Some people may fear that paying attention to their painful feelings will lead to being taken over by those feelings. But that consequence is much more likely as a result of trying to deny them. To pay attention to them is not only to respect them but to be open to the possibility that they may have something to tell us that we need to hear, that they may be prodding us in new, more creative, and more fulfilling directions. To deny the pain, to try to pretend it away, is to close the door on the potential for transformation that it may offer. It is to deny the time-honored truth that sometimes the only way out of pain is through it. It is to refuse to consider the possibility that through the process we may find greater depth, breadth, and strength in ourselves than we had previously known.

It would be surprising if we were *not* troubled in the wake of a job crisis—especially if it involved the loss of a job or the failure of a business. For there are many positive things about employment—even employment we do not especially like. In many cases, for example, it has a social dimension. It provides a regular opportunity for the challenge and the pleasure of interacting with others. As such, it keeps us from being alone too much while giving us something to do. The discomforts of being without employment include not only the sense of loneliness that may be involved, but also the fact that we are forced to concentrate not so much on *doing* as on *being*.

Naturally, employment brings in money—which not only allows for buying the things we need but also is, as I have noted, the primary way in which our culture assesses value. It therefore gives us a sense of control, of security. It allows us to keep some of the painful realities of life at bay—or at least to feel that we can do so.

Employment also gives us a sense of place. That truth is implicit in the fact that we often refer to our paid work as our occupation—almost literally the place we occupy. To be without that sense of place, that sense of security, is no small matter. It leaves a void, an emptiness. As one of the men I talked with said of himself, "I feel out of the mainstream, on the sidelines."

Without job work we may feel, quite literally, out of place—out of a place in which to exist and feel needed. In some cases, apparently, that sense of loss is so great that people cannot face it realistically. I have heard, for example, of individuals who for months on end have left their homes daily, briefcase or lunch pail in hand, pretending to go to jobs that no longer existed for them.

These examples are added confirmation of the fact that at one level of selfhood a sense of place is very important—and that changing places is not easy. Many outplacement firms are aware of this, and, no doubt in an effort to accommodate it, provide some kind of office for their clients—a desk, perhaps a cubicle, a telephone, the shared services of a secretary, and the like. And, in the framework of searching for another job, that kind of feeling and appearance of continuity may well be important.

Remember, however, that we are discussing two kinds of transition here. One involves moving from one job or type of paid employment to another. It is the transition which is the concern of our ego—that part of our self whose priorities are the practical, the social, the economic. It is a very real transition, often one that is difficult and a threat to our self-esteem. It may involve letting go of that which represents one of the greatest, if not the greatest, single-time investment of our lives.

Leaving a job leaves a hole in our life, and we want to fill that hole. And, unless we think about it, we may simply assume that the only way of filling it is to find another way to make a living. Even if we may have felt vague feelings of emptiness when we were in the job, we hasten—sometimes out of necessity but not always—to look for another, usually as much like the one we left as possible.

That kind of thinking will probably be most strongly experienced by people who have used job work to fill every available "space" in their lives. Some individuals achieve that objective with one job. Others may take second jobs—not out of financial need but out of a *perceived* need to "stay busy."

But some people find themselves dissatisfied with the self-as-job kind of identity. Some people, probably many people, want more—which leads us to the second kind of transition. For some, the need may be felt only a vague inkling. But for others it is much clearer. They are ready, or at least willing, to let go of their traditional identity. They are choosing to destroy the illusions of job work before they are destroyed by them. They are prepared to confront and accept the deeper parts of themselves, including their vulnerability—the spaces in their lives that obsessive busyness simply can't fill. They are finding the courage to re-vision themselves, to re-map their lives, to get in touch with a new dimension of self and develop a new sense of who they are. They are becoming more open to knowing themselves—not only in the destinations associated with making a living but in the process involved in making a life.

In my conversations with people who have made or are making a change involving employment I found that quite a number want to learn to see themselves in a deeper and broader perspective than is provided by paid employment alone. In some cases, that effort has had to parallel working with some urgency at finding another job. In other instances, however, people had come to recognize their deeper needs in advance of a job change and they factored in a way to deal with them.

One such person was Brian, the former university administrator we met earlier, who felt such a loss of identity when he was laid off. Part of Brian's severance package included a healthy amount for the services of an outplacement firm of his choice. But prior to his termination, Brian had begun to do some work on himself and, initially, he thought he would continue that kind of pursuit in the context of career transition counselling. But what he encountered was something different.

"I went up to this relocation counselor, and they were really nice people but I think I was quite confusing for them, because they were really only able to talk about job searches. I thought this would be another kind of counseling situation and we could talk about things in general. But as I got partway through the process I began to realize that what they were best at doing I wasn't interested in."

What Brian was interested in was a new slant on living rather than a new way of making a living. He has found the latter, incidentally, through working for his wife, who owns a small publishing company. He described the period between leaving the university and starting to work for his wife as "a sort of drifting period. It wasn't very focused. Then I drifted into my wife's office and she said, 'You know, you can come down here as often as you want.' Then I got a contract for her, then I started working on it."

Not everyone would be comfortable with Brian's approach, of course. And it would not be possible—or at least not as feasible—for many people. But the point is that he was exercising options which were out of the ordinary—and which he previously had not considered. They were options having more to do with him as a person than as a breadwinner. Making the change was not easy, but for Brian it has been worth it.

"I think that I'm not only going to live longer, I think that I'm going to live more creatively. I think there are a lot fewer knee-jerk responses in my daily life than there used to be. When I was going to work, I don't think I ever realized that I had a lot of options, nor did I see myself as having enough nerve to accept them."

A woman I'll call Judith experienced a transition that is in some ways similar to Brian's, but also very different. For more than ten years after her graduation from university, Judith was on an upwardly mobile career track with a pharmaceutical company. But there was a problem.

"I just knew that I didn't like what I was doing. I wasn't happy at the end of the day, making a deal and knowing that there was going to be a contract for the next several years to provide products to a customer. Having the thing be signed, sealed and delivered didn't give me a kick. I knew people who got a kick out of successfully closing a deal, but I didn't. No matter how many zeros were attached that didn't do it for me."

For a number of years Judith persevered, however, telling herself that if the description or the location of the job changed a bit, she would be happy. At one point she was relocated to the headquarters of the parent company, which "meant that I'd be getting into the mainstream of running the overall operation. I got moved and I fully expected I would convince myself that this change was for the good and that I was doing this for life. I bought a place close to my office downtown and thought,

'Oh, here I am, this single woman living in the heart of a beautiful city, sort of the world is at my feet.' I moved and after three weeks I already recognized my unhappiness."

After giving her new situation six months, Judith decided to leave the company and, having set aside enough money to live on for a year, she relocated. And during that time she did nothing "productive"—which was not easy for her.

"It wasn't that easy an adjustment. It took until the end of the first year, when I knew I was going to get a job, for me to be comfortable with the concept of hanging out. I was not comfortable with downtime. I was not comfortable *having* time. I didn't know how to be at peace with myself. That's what I learned. I had no clue that it was okay to do nothing. I didn't *know* how to do nothing. I felt guilty about doing nothing, so I was constantly trying to fill my time with activity. Today I really savor my time to do nothing, but otherwise I don't think about it. Then I was always thinking about it and feeling very uncomfortable."

One way Judith found to occupy her time during that year was motorcycling around the area where she was living. That interest, which she shared with her boyfriend, led at the end of her year of transition to their opening a motorcycle shop. At the time of my interview with her, the shop was in its second year of operation and Judith was starting to feel that they had survived the startup period and were becoming somewhat knowledgeable about running a business.

As probably can be surmised from the information included in their stories, Brian and Judith are of different generations. He is in his mid-50s; she is in her early 30s. He is male; she is female. Whatever their differences, however, they both took their need for a new kind of transition seriously and realized that it went deeper than a change of employment. They recognized that it had to do not only with their outer circumstances but with inner development. They were willing to let go of overattachment to the self that defines itself in social and economic terms and to begin making conscious contact with a deeper part of the self.

To some extent, of course, the point one has reached in life will have a bearing on how one responds to an employment crisis. Which side of "mid-life" one is on may well affect one's outlook. But as noted earlier, our development doesn't always occur according to schedule. Sometimes the challenges of life cut across chronology. Some young people face challenges thought to be more properly the province of mature adults. And some individuals in their forties, fifties, and older are still dealing with the issues of adolescence.

Irrespective of one's age, the fact is that the invitation to go deeper into one's life and experience is always present in a crisis. In the case of unemployment, the crisis itself involves letting go of a job. But the invitation may well have to do with letting go of one's image—of how one perceives of one's self.

An example of what I am talking about can be seen in the story of Buckminster Fuller—the inventor of the geodesic dome. In the 1920s, a business venture of Fuller's collapsed soon after the death of his infant daughter, and he was devastated to the point of considering suicide. Instead, he committed what he called "egocide."* By that term he meant surrendering to the idea that if he attended to his duties on behalf of humanity by utilizing his gifts in the fields of design and human ecology, his needs would be met. He freed himself from overattachment to some of the concerns that had been sapping his energy, and so was able to contribute to humanity in an extraordinary way.

There is no way of knowing for sure, of course, it seems likely that the unusually full and productive life led by Buckminster Fuller was related to that pivotal decision in his life. For that kind of letting go allows us to see the invitations implicit in the challenges that confront us and to find and claim new vision, purpose, and creativity. It is more than positive thinking; it is affirmation of self in depth. And it almost invariably involves a sense of dislocation—the awareness that we are leaving whatever place we are used to, physically, spiritually, or both, and venturing into new territory.

So one of the feelings that is invariably a companion on that journey is grief—which we sometimes think has to do only with death. But it is a normal human response to any loss. It has to do with life's ongoing cycle of dying and being reborn, of loss and renewal, of the old giving way to the new. It is part of the "necessary losses" Judith Viorst has written about in her book of the same name and which are an integral part of our growth and development. As a friend of mine said recently, "If a person is not feeling grief over something, he or she isn't alive." It is how we respond to that reality, to that process, that determines the fullness—or the emptiness—of our lives.

Part of the problem is that we think of grief as something totally negative—something to be denied, to be avoided. But grief is an essential part of the healing process. Just as physical wounds heal by growing new tissue—which can be a painful process—so do wounds of the heart, soul, and spirit encourage growth. The emotional pain that comes with it is the way that some of our usually silent parts have of communicating. To know ourselves fully is to pay attention to those parts. And if we pay attention carefully enough, we may find that healing is an implicit part of the pain. We may find that saying goodbye is essential to saying hello—to getting on with the next phase of our lives.

Grieving is a process which encompasses a number of feelings, including shame, regret, loneliness, anger, and fear. Almost invariably those feelings hover around us, unnamed, flitting in and out of our hearts, minds, and guts. If we are to know ourselves as fully as possible we need to name them, get acquainted with them and try to determine if they have something valuable to tell us about who we are and who we can become.

All of these feelings may seem to suggest woundedness. But it is important to remember that wounds can also heal—and that we may be "put back together" better than we were before. We are talking not about an "instant fix" but about transformation—which is a very different thing. We are talking about strengthening the foundation and the infrastructure of our lives, rather than just papering over the cracks. We are talking about real work in the midst of a job work crisis.

Shame, for example, has to do with feeling bad about who we are—or, more specifically, about feeling that we don't measure up to the expectations we have of ourselves and/or the expectations we think others have of us. Shame and guilt are often used synonymously, but they are in fact different. Guilt has to do with an action, something that is an outcome of will. Shame has to do with our very being, with a sense of incompleteness, with the limitations of will. Shame is about feelings of inadequacy—a sense of being less than we should be.

Brian, for example, remembers his feelings at the time of his job loss: "You know, you obviously screwed up or this wouldn't have happened, so there was this feeling of humiliation that I shouldn't have got myself into this situation. I mean I understood what the hierarchy was all about, and so I must have been a pretty willful, irrational person to, in effect, have *earned* this letter dismissing me. "

Brian's experience also illustrates the fact that feelings of shame may have nothing to do with having done anything bad in the immoral or unethical sense. Like most people who lose their jobs, Brian was not guilty of any wrongdoing. Yet he felt ashamed of himself. And the same kind of thing can be true in other areas. There is nothing *wrong,* for example, with being in poor health, with being poorly educated, or with crying in public. Yet people often experience shame in connection with those things and sundry others of the same sort.

The most natural reaction to shame is to run and hide, to try to cover one's vulnerability. But we should remember that shame is an integral part of being human. It goes hand in hand with our capacity for self-consciousness, with our ability to know ourselves. To pretend to be without shame is to pretend to be more or less than human.

Confronting our shame can be very painful, of course, just as confronting any of the feelings I am talking about here can be painful. It is in that confrontation, however, that we find a new basis for connection with others—a basis founded in recognition and acceptance of our common humanity. It is through honestly acknowledging, confronting, and indeed, embracing our shame—in a safe and supportive environment—that we transform it and discover who we truly are.

In the words of Helen Merrill Lynd, author of *On Shame and the Search For Identity,* "Shame interrupts any unquestioning, unaware sense of oneself." And, she goes further to argue that "experiences of shame if confronted full in the face may throw an unexpected light on who one is and point the way toward who one may become."* In other words, confronting our shame can help us to break through our perfectionism. Doing so can move us toward self-forgiveness (even if we have done nothing wrong), toward the discovery that it is truly all right to be human.

Fear is another common feeling during times of uncertainty. In the case of unemployment, the fear may have to do primarily with meeting our survival needs and those of our family. But our fear may also spring from other wells, which may be worth thinking about. For example, fear may have to do with loss of status, with concern about rejection by people who are significant in our lives, with failure or lack of success, with awareness of our mortality. Fear may overlap with shame—as, for example, with Brian who admits that one of his fears was how to explain the fact that he had lost his job.

But whatever the source of the fear, listening to it will almost invariably tell us something about ourselves that we did not know or have tried to deny. Which helps to explain the opinion, attributed to pioneer psychotherapist Carl Jung by another therapist, Robert Johnson, that the thing a person fears most is the point of opportunity for his or her next area of development. *

The greatest problem with anger—another painful feeling that is part and parcel of grief and loss—is that we may try to deal with it in ways that are destructive to ourselves, others, or both. Those hurtful actions tend to happen when we try to deny anger. Which is not to say that we should let it take over, but it does mean we need to feel it and acknowledge it for what it is—a natural response to loss that can be a constructive part of the transition process. Anger can become a resource in helping us to say goodbye. And, constructively channeled, it may give us the energy and determination we need to confront whatever challenges are involved in getting on with our lives.

It is also useful to try to identify both the reasons for our anger and the focal point of it. Fear often underlies anger, and as with fear, we can often learn a lot by listening to our anger. It can be a resource not only for dealing constructively with the challenges confronting us but for getting to know more about ourselves.

Regret is another feeling common to difficult times, including those brought on by employment crises. And there are several things we need to keep in mind here. One is that a life without regret wouldn't be worth living. To be fully alive is to make choices—even not to make choices is to make a choice. And, life being what it is, our choices don't always turn out the way we want. At times of crisis, when we feel disappointment and a sense of failure, we always imagine that things would have been better if we'd made different choices. This is far from certain, and, besides, we can only make our choices with the information available at the time they are made.

One thing that exacerbates regret as a normal part of living is the fact that we live in a culture which worships success—which bombards us with glittering images of alleged success and encourages the belief that it is possible to "do it all" and "have it all." And our regret may have about it a dual edge: we may regret both that we have not succeeded as well as we have been led to believe we *should* have, and that we bought into the values of others at the expense of our own priorities. As painful as regret is, therefore, it can help to put us in touch with who we truly are and what we value most. It is never too late for that knowledge to be valuable.

Loneliness is yet another of the "valley" feelings that I want to touch on here. It goes hand in hand with feelings of loss and shame, and it may be especially acute if we are feeling betrayed and disillusioned. At times we feel lonely no matter how many people are around. As with the other feelings being identified here, it would be a mistake to try to deny that reality.

But it is also important to remember that loneliness is one of the essential polarities of our existence. On the one hand, we share a common humanity with all of our brothers and sisters. On the other, no two of us are alike. Each of us is unique. We can only do our own growing and there are times when feeling separate and alone is an essential part of our growth. It is part of the individuation process, part of "leaving the nest"—whether the word "nest" represents our home, our family, or some other situation or location in which we have grown comfortable.

Loneliness is part of the space we occupy after having said goodbye but before reaching the next point on our journey where we can truly say hello—the place at which we find ourselves after having left behind our self-as-job identity but before having realized a new sense of self. It is part of the inner strengthening which can come when we experience betrayal and let go of some of our illusions.

Accepting our loneliness does not mean that we forego healing connections or that we try to do everything for ourselves. It simply means that it is part of the process whereby we are able to affirm our true interdependence with others and to become open to new and more meaningful connectedness. By embracing our loneliness we may actually become better able to embrace community more fully.

All of the feelings I've described are painful. Thus we want to avoid them, to deny them, or at the very least to try to fix them. Our compulsive attachment to job work can be a way of trying to do any or all of those things. And I assuredly am not advocating that we give in to them in a way that leads to despair—though at times we may feel close to that point. But to fail to honor our uncomfortable feelings is to fail to honor significant parts of ourselves. It is to fail to learn from them, to fail to discover through them pathways to new resourcefulness and strength. It *is* possible to acknowledge and process them in a way that transforms them and us. It is not an easy way; it requires considerable courage. But, as I suggested earlier, there is some truth in the adage that the only real way out of pain is through it.

One person who experienced that reality is Leon, the former accounts manager we met, who admitted that his job loss left him feeling completely and utterly devastated—so much so that he considered suicide. Leon went through relocation counseling and group therapy and he began the process of getting to know himself better. As so often happens, however, it was not a one-step process. In fact, it involved finding another job, losing it as a result of the recession, and then being forced into retirement in his mid-50s.

Nevertheless, Leon sees the process he has gone through as one which has been beneficial. He described, for example, how his priorities have changed for the better. After the job loss in 1988, he recalled, "my focus was still just on getting another job. I hadn't learned what I know today. I spent eighty percent of my time, my energy and my thoughts towards finding another position; fifteen to twenty percent of my time went to dealing with my anger, my loss of self-esteem, and related things. "

Leon admitted that he approached his new job in much the same way as the old one. "I immediately became a company man. I again put in more time on the job than my family thought was reasonable, and I was still accepting responsibility for things that were happening that I had no control over. I guess I was still trying to use a job to get a feeling of satisfaction for other things."

Now, however, more than four years after losing his first job, Leon sees things differently. While admitting that he would like to be working and that he feels a little "out of the mainstream of things," he summarized his present view by saying,"My approach to life now is that a job would be a very small part of overall living. A job allows you to live in a way that can be fulfilling, whereas my attitude before was that the job was everything, and that anything else was secondary. If everything was fine at the job, then everything else would automatically be fine, too. My outlook now is that, fine, it would be nice to have a job, but it won't come before me and before my family and before a number of other things. Believe me, it's taken a lot of years to come to that point. And I know I recognize those things rather late in life. But I'm glad that I do."

What often happens, of course, is that people make a change, thinking that the transition will be of relatively short duration. We feel that we will locate another job, or get a business off the ground, or whatever—and in short order. And then reality begins to set in. The severance package is exhausted, unemployment insurance dries up, one's spouse has to get a job for the first time, credit cards have been used up to or past their limits, the mortgage has to be renewed, Christmas is coming up and you know that the kids, however understanding and supportive they are trying to be, are inevitably going to be disappointed at what's under the tree—if there is a tree. And some people reading this, I am sure, would say that the scene I have painted is just the beginning.

In fact, the transition process is usually slow, often painfully so—as I know from my own experience. In 1978, I left a secure, salaried position, thinking that a job change might somehow cause a problem I was experiencing to go away and that I could then get on with my life expeditiously. As things have unfolded, however, the transition that was begun more than a decade ago is only now coming to a conclusion—if, indeed, that is the right word.

And, in the course of "getting on with my life," other significant things also happened: I finally decided to deal with the problem confronting me rather than continuing to deny it; both of my parents died; my children graduated from high school, went to another city to continue their education, and then to work; my daughter married; I was involved in several business ventures and came very near to bankruptcy. It has not been a linear process but one that has been spiral in nature and has had spirals within spirals.

In cases where transitions do seem to happen quickly, they are almost always the culmination of a preparatory period that had been going on for some time. For example, Brian had experienced marriage problems a few years prior to the termination of his job as a university administrator, which had led him to begin doing some inner work. As he explained, "I think I got some awareness that there were people out there who were standing ready to help me whenever I was experiencing some kind of trauma in my life. And they were available to me with my wife or without my wife. They were just there." As a result of this realization, he was more ready to make significant changes when he lost his job than he might otherwise have been. And the same sort of thing was true of some of the other people I interviewed; earlier events turned out to be part of an ongoing transition.

Whatever the specifics, any transition of the sort we are talking about often if not always involves uncertainty and discouragement. We feel we have lost our bearings, our place, and we aren't sure how we will find our way either back to where we were or forward.

We need not be surprised by these feelings. For while the great stories we are heirs to remind us that there is growth and strength and healing to be found in the transition process, they also remind us that the process is anything but quick and easy.

One of the better known stories of that sort is the one about Odysseus, king of Ithaca and hero of the Trojan War, which was fought in ancient Greece. As you may remember, the real drama started when, after using his prowess to defeat Troy (he was the one behind the wooden horse scheme), Odysseus and his men gave in to the temptation to fight just one more battle—which should have been an easy win. But in fact they lost. And thus began a journey of many years during which he was buffeted by storms, challenged by many enemies, and lost all of his ships and men. He was stripped of his pride, and had to unlearn old ways, which previously had worked well, and to learn new ones—which included confronting his vulnerability. At one point he had to do nothing for an extended period, as a time to heal and to prepare himself for the final stage of his return home. He had to let go of an identity based on something he had been very good at doing (winning battles) in order to make his way home and become a more complete human being.

The point of such stories is the reminder that, no matter how stuck we may seem, how much a victim of external events, there can be a healing, strengthening, and transforming process going on in our depths. What is vital is that we find the courage to face the reality of the process—particularly when we feel that we are stuck, when we feel that all our efforts are futile, when we feel that we are of little or no value.

The kind of process I am talking about here has to do with what might be termed "soul work." The word "soul" is admittedly hard to define, but, as I am using it here, it refers not to some *thing* but to a dimension of life. Psychotherapist and former Catholic monk Thomas Moore talks about it as "a dimension of experiencing life and ourselves" and as having to do with "depth, value, relatedness, heart, and personal substance."* It is through soul that we are connected with the eternal. It is the soul dimension of life which has to do with meaning and with value.

Soul is sometimes used in a religious context, but it is not limited to that framework. We speak, for example, of music which has soul. And we speak of individuals who have soul—meaning not so much that they are religious as that they have learned through their experience to affirm life in its totality, both its heights and its depths, both its clarity and its mystery.

Soul work is part of any kind of initiatory experience, any kind of letting go and moving on type of experience. It is involved any time we reframe our life, any time we revision the map of our journey. Soul has to do with the transformative power of valleys as well as mountaintops. I sometimes think of it as the distilling part of our being.

The struggle involved in developing identity and self-esteem which go beyond job work has to do with interaction between ego, soul, and self. To be overattached to a job, or to anything else, is to live out of a disproportionate ego base. It is to assume a false self and to be without needed power. It may give the illusion of success, but it actually keeps us from growing and from gaining a fuller understanding of who we are.

To be freed from that false self—or, perhaps more accurately, that limited self—is to know a new kind of strength and power. That is so whether the issue involved is work, drugs, personal relationships or whatever. At the same time, breaking away from that limited self allows for development of an appropriate kind of ego strength, which has to do with boundaries and individuation and which is a vital part of human development and personal authenticity. It is an ego strength that comes from within, from one's true self—from one's soul.

One word I mentioned in my review of the troubling feelings likely to accompany difficult transitions is the word "failure"—which, as we all know, can be felt in many ways in connection with employment crises. "Failure" deserves our attention—which includes reminding ourselves that it is almost always a subjective judgment. Seldom if ever is it a statement of fact. We do, however, experience feelings of failure.

When it comes to employment, failure is most often understood as job loss or the collapse of a business. Sometimes, however, we may be very successful outwardly but feel we have failed because our success is not in line with our sense of calling. Or we may experience a sense of failure if the results we see in our work do not match the effort we have put in—if we reluctantly come to the conclusion that the dream we have pursued, whether it has been security, a particular position, or wealth, is not going to be realized. And, given the fact that we live in a culture which virtually worships success, there may well be other configurations of failure which gnaw at us.

Whatever the particulars, we need to keep in mind that it is failure which keeps us tied to our soul. According to psychotherapist Thomas Moore, whom I cited earlier, our lofty aims sometimes have to be spoiled a bit if their creative potential is to be realized. And he goes on to argue that "by appreciating failure with imagination, we reconnect it to success."* Failure can thus be a refining tool—or, to put it another way, a great teacher.

The point is that while our sense of failure may bring us to a perceived dead end, any time we come up against such a place we are ready to begin a new phase of our journey. As Jungian therapist Robert Johnson puts it, "it is when the unstoppable bullet hits the impenetrable wall" that we have our deepest experiences.* It does not matter how the awareness comes. The crucial thing is that it *does* come—and that we respond to the invitation implicit in that kind of awareness. For it is when we come to such a point that a potentially deepening experience is at hand.

People experience grief, shame, anger, fear, regret, loneliness, failure, and other painful feelings in various ways, with varying degrees of intensity. There is no way of attaching a standard formula, meaning, or message to each of them. But we do need to listen to what they are saying. We need to accept that what is called for is more than "fixing" them—which often means denying them and their potential significance. We need to enter into them and be prepared to learn from them. In the process it may help to keep a few things in mind.

One, which I mentioned earlier, is that we have to say goodbye in order to be able to say hello. Endings are important. Implicit in every ending is a new beginning, even if it is hidden from us at the time. We therefore need to honor goodbyes. We need to honor grief.

Which is what we do with physical death; we have a ceremony, which we call a funeral. But we don't have to limit our goodbye ceremonies to funerals. They can be appropriate in many other settings—including the loss of employment. And so, if you have lost a job, or even if the job you have has lost its meaning, you may want to devise a ceremony of your own as part of letting go of it—or letting go of its significance to you. For example, you might simply want to write down a description of the job—its good parts and its bad ones—and then tear up the paper, burn it, or even bury it.

Another thing to keep in mind, even as part of the saying goodbye process, is the importance of knowing not only what we are leaving behind—which is a good reason for writing out a summary of the job and disposing of it—but also remembering what we still have. Sometimes, what you left behind may seem to you highly desirable. In other instances it may be that it is quite the opposite.

Brian, for example, now feels that the work environment he left was highly toxic. And he also has found that he did not leave all of himself there. (If you feel that you have left yourself behind with your job, you may want to make a list of those parts of you that are still intact—perhaps, for example, your health, your skills and abilities, your sense of humor, the people who are significant in your life, things that energize you or have at times in your life energized you, and more.)

The third thing we should be aware of is that every crisis includes an invitation. In the words of Jon Kabat-Zinn, Associate Professor of Medicine and Director of the Stress Reduction Program at the University of Massachusetts Medical School, healing comes through facing the "full catastrophe" of life and finding that resources for strength and transformation are offered by the raw materials of our experience—our own "catastrophe," whatever it may be.*

We should also remember that "falling apart" is sometimes part of the process. In the view of a psychiatrist by the name of Frederic Flach, it may even be the most appropriate response to some stressful situations. He is not saying that falling apart should be considered the norm. Nor should it result in behavior which is destructive of oneself or others. Rather, Flach is saying that in some circumstances, failure to fall apart may be as unhealthy as the failure to find a new way to grow following a crisis.*

Above all, remember that reaching out for help is a sign of strength and maturity—not weakness—and that falling apart does not have to be permanent. There are some kinds of brokenness which, when healed, leave us stronger than we were before.

Finally, I suggest we keep in mind that things are happening even when they don't seem to be happening. I recall, for example, hearing an interview with a man who was recovering from a stroke. The person talking to him asked if he thought he was improving. Speaking slowly, his speech still affected by what had happened to him, he said that he sometimes wasn't sure but that people told him he was. And he added that he guessed that was so because sometimes he found himself doing things which he had not been able to do a few weeks or a few months earlier.

Just as was true for that man, our growing and becoming process is often not obvious except in retrospect. And it is seldom straight. If we were to diagram it, the line would undoubtedly zig and zag a good deal, much like the kind of path often taken by children on their way home from school. It is often marked by detours, some of our own choosing, some forced upon us. In a sense, the process is never complete—although there are almost always resting places along the way. If we are only concerned with trying a "fix" of one kind or another, we are likely to miss that which is of more lasting value. We may be so concerned with the outcome that we miss the values waiting to be discovered in the process.

To make the kind of transition I am talking about requires a peculiar mixture of effort on the one hand and surrender on the other. It is not easy. It does entail risk—just as do many things which involve the whole person. Earlier in life, for example, we felt much the same kind of apprehension at learning to walk and to ride a bicycle. Just as then, we continue to pass from time to time through periods of feeling unprotected, vulnerable.

Sometimes those are very long periods; almost invariably they seem to be a long ones. And yet, as countless people who have recovered from traumas and illnesses can testify, there is a way to find strength through facing pain and vulnerability.

We are all subject to a number of very powerful influences which contribute to the widespread belief that selfhood is synonymous with what a person does for a living, and that attachment to one's role in the workplace is the only legitimate basis of self-esteem. That viewpoint, as I have emphasized, is a limited and a limiting one.

But there are other ways of viewing oneself and the world, other stances. There are choices—healing choices. The most basic one has to do with willingness to move from a definition of self based solely on what is "out there" to one derived mainly from within ourselves.

Most of the time life goes along routinely enough—or at least the bumps aren't rough enough to attract our attention for any extended time. But then something happens. It may be a health crisis, a relationship crisis, or some other type of crisis. Or it may not be a crisis at all, at least not in terms of any outward signs. We may simply sense that things aren't right in a way that is as powerful as it is subtle. Whatever the circumstances, we are arrested, we are brought up short, we find ourselves attending to questions which we had been ignoring, or which we thought had been answered long ago.

One of the things that can bring us up short is an employment crisis. It may be unemployment; it may be the promotion we had been working for but which didn't come; it may be a business failure. It may simply be a sense that, however well we are doing, what we are doing isn't right for us. Whatever the cause, we are forced to reframe, to rethink, to take a fresh look at ourselves and our journey.

Or at least we are given that opportunity—which is what I am trying to draw attention to in this book. We can, of course, pass up the opportunity—or fail to be even aware of it. We may be fortunate (or unfortunate) in quickly finding a new job or in convincing ourselves that we will find renewed satisfaction by throwing ourselves more frenetically into the one we have. Or we may feel that the answer is on the next rung up the ladder or on one parallel to the one we had been climbing.

But the alternative is to see in an employment crisis an opportunity for personal and spiritual growth. The alternative, as I have been suggesting, is to take at least a bit of time to step aside, to review our lives (literally, to *re-view* them) and to discover or rediscover some parts of ourselves that may have gotten lost along the way. If we find it necessary to do so, we should not be surprised or ashamed. For the fact is that most of us are programmed from an early age for life on a treadmill. But it doesn't have to be that way. We are given opportunities throughout our lives to reprogram, to discover and implement new options.

Transitions are seldom easy. Navigating them may mean radically changing our view of ourselves and our world. In one way or another, they require that we give up old ways of thinking, let go of many preconceived notions, and find faith to review and reorder our lives.

That kind of change requires both honesty and courage. But it is possible. There are resources available—including the power that comes from knowing your own story, from tapping into your creativity, and from finding strength and purpose through connectedness with others. In the pages ahead I will be offering suggestions as to how you can discover these and other resources for yourself and learn to live and work with greater freedom, confidence, and integrity.

Chapter Three

SELFHOOD BEYOND THE RESUME

One of our most enduring gifts from ancient Greece is the admonition "Know thyself." That piece of advice, which has been emphasized time and time again over the centuries, is important at any time in a person's life. But we should pay special attention to it during times of transition, crisis, and challenge.

For self-knowledge is directly related to healthy self-esteem. And knowing ourselves in depth can help us make a life fitted to our standards, values, and priorities rather than solely to those of others. Even when we have to conform, which we all do to some extent, knowing who we are allows us to be aware of why we are doing so, and to claim as best we can what is truly important to us. Self-knowledge can help us find confidence from within rather than from relying too much on external factors.

We can come to realize, moreover, that behind the roles we play are many values and concerns, which continue to change and evolve and which represent parts of ourselves as important as our "public" self. In fact, in the process of getting to know ourselves, we may discover that we are defined more by parts of ourselves which have been neglected than by those which we have paid attention to. In the words of the pioneer psychotherapist Carl Jung, we may realize that there are "Many—far too many—aspects of life which should...have been experienced" but which in fact lie "among dusty memories."*

Unfortunately, we tend to ignore the importance of self-knowledge. When we do pay attention to it, we often do so in a somewhat circumscribed way. All career transition counseling, for example, includes some attention to the matter of self-knowledge. For the most part, however, it is geared toward a definite end—getting another job. This kind of self-knowledge is designed to help you determine how you can best fit into the marketplace: what kinds of skills and services you have to offer, the kind of setting in which you are most comfortable working, and the kind of income and responsibility to which you might aspire.

That kind of information is valuable. Although it is focused on job-finding, it can offer understanding that goes beyond the workplace and merges with self-knowledge of a deeper sort. But it is not the whole story. *For to know yourself fully is to know not only what you want to do but who you are and who you want to be.*

To know yourself in that way is to know more than fits into a resume. We must start with the understanding that it may be a good thing to "lose" an old sense of identity if it is one-dimensional. Then we can open the way to know ourselves through a process that can be transformative. That process happens by way of getting in touch with our own stories and our own myths.

Those words—"story" and "myth"—are ones which we recognize as important but still continue to devalue. We accept them as significant but we tend to dismiss them as having little to do with "real" life. We may accept, for example, that stories are something appropriate for children at bedtime. But lurking in the back of our minds is also the notion that stories are not really true. In some settings, "telling a story" is synonymous with telling a lie or a fib. And "myth" evokes many of the same attitudes—perhaps even stronger ones.

We often think of a myth as a kind of fairy tale—perhaps about gods and goddesses, to be sure, but a fairy tale nonetheless. And, because myths are not "true"—not factual and scientific—we assume that they are of no particular value.

As I am using the word "myth," however, it has a different and much deeper meaning. For myths are anything but false. As defined by Stanley Krippner in the book *Personal Mythology,* myths are "the models by which human beings code and organize their perceptions, feelings, thoughts, and actions."* That is, they provide us with a framework which can help us understand ourselves and the world in which we live.

Our ancient ancestors understood better than we do the importance of myths and of stories as a primary means by which they are conveyed. They told stories about the creation of the world, about great floods, about the origins of toil and the travail of childbirth, about the interactions of goddesses and gods with each other and with human beings, about why it is that winter is bleak and spring brings renewal of life. Those stories had a mythic dimension in that they were told to give understanding, not only about the "how" of things and events but also about their meaning and purpose. They helped people connect with the world in which they lived, even if many parts of it were essentially mysterious.

Stories have always been a prime part of the identity of peoples and tribes and nations. Over the centuries, for example, the Hebrew people have kept alive their distinctive identity by recounting their history as a people who were rescued from slavery and delivered to a land that had special significance for them. Modern nations have stories which help to form their mythology. In the United States, for example, youngsters grow up hearing stories associated with the American Revolution—the Boston Tea Party, the midnight ride of Paul Revere, and the like. In Canada, stories of that kind are fewer, but there are elements of cultural mythology surrounding things such as the Royal Canadian Mounted Police and the driving of the last railroad spike which connected the country from coast to coast.

In the same way, every family is the collective embodiment of its own myths—the history, values, and characteristics which separate, say, the Harrison clan from the Cheavens clan. That fact often comes as a rude shock to newly-married individuals, each of whom brings to the marriage definite ideas about how things should be done—for example, how Christmas should be celebrated. In response to that fact, psychologists who work with couples often help them learn to communicate better with each other by becoming aware of the patterns and values and ways of doing things—the myths—of their respective families of origin.

These examples remind us that storytelling and myth making are what mark us as humans. To be human is both to tell stories and to be the repository of stories. The stories that we absorb from our families, our teachers, and our culture combine with our myriad experiences to create the framework of meaning in which we operate. In our culture, one very significant part of that framework is the notion that a person is defined primarily by his or her relationship to paid work. That is a myth; it is a habitual way of seeing things, of thinking about things.

In addition to collective myths, however, we also have our individual myths. Our personal myths are rooted in our own experience but are also a reflection of the mythology held by the culture we live in and the families we are part of. There is, therefore, an inevitable tension between the worldview we are given and the one we devise for ourselves. The challenge for each of us is to engage in an ongoing revision of the myths which guide us. The challenge is to make our myths appropriate and true for ourselves.

That challenge should not be taken lightly. It is not an overnight project. Nor is it an invitation to cast off all restraints and behave irresponsibly. It is, rather, an opportunity to gain a deeper, more authentic awareness of who we are. It is an invitation to know ourselves in a new way, which can be freeing and empowering, to join actively in authoring our own script, and thus to claim appropriate *author*ity over our own lives.

I am not suggesting that we try to control everything that happens to us—which is quite impossible. Rather, we should try to respond to events from a center of awareness of who we are and what is important to us. We do not control the winds of fate but we can set our sails in the best way possible to take us in the direction we want to go. We can take seriously the choices which are ours.

Doing so requires a willingness to reinvent, reframe, and revision ourselves on an ongoing basis. Perhaps more accurately, it requires re-visioning the map of our lives, even redrawing it—recharting our course. That possibility is implicit in an often-used metaphor for living that I have already mentioned—the journey.

It doesn't rule out stopping places, plateaus, even oases. But it does suggest that our stories, our myths, our *selves* are at once known and in the process of being discovered, are at once developed and in the process of unfolding.

Fortunately, we are starting to recover the importance of myth and story and the value of discovering who we are by way of them. We are coming to realize that stories can be true, that there is truth embodied in fiction even if it is a truth different from the scientific kind.

A number of developments have contributed to our reawakened awareness of the power of story. They include the the emergence in 1935 of Alcoholics Anonymous and the mutual help movement it has spawned, the publication of Alex Haley's book *Roots* and the television series based on it, and the increasing accessibility of psychotherapy of various sorts. The common denominator in all of those examples, it seems to me, is the power of stories to deepen and transform our understanding of ourselves.

And so it is that we need to get in touch with our own stories—with their mixture of straight paths and detours, their record of successes and failures large and small. We need to be aware, moreover, of the ways in which the stories of others have imprinted themselves on our lives and have melded, for good or bad, into our own stories. For by doing so, we open ourselves to the discovery that *we are truly defined not by our labels but by our stories.*

As a friend of mine likes to put it, "who we are is where we've been." To which I simply would add that who we are is also how we interpret and respond to where we've been. For our stories are not simply factual accounts of events. They are our interpretation, our understanding, of the happenings and developments that have led us to the present moment.

Let's come back to the story of Odysseus. Asked to tell who he is, Odysseus told his story, which is essentially the narrative we know as the *Odyssey*. Through his experiences and his retelling of them, he identifies himself; he becomes the author of his own identity. He comes to know who he is—which is a very different and much deeper individual than the general/warrior/political leader he had known himself to be at the start of his journey.

In like manner, if we are to discover that we are truly more than our jobs—more than any one of the roles we play—we must rediscover the power of story. Each person must reclaim his or her personal mythology. And, in the process, we must discover that *identity is a journey—not a destination.*

Telling our stories can make us aware of the significant points of our journey to date, some of which we may have neglected to notice on the way. An employment crisis can thus become an opportunity to explore paths we may previously have passed by. We can find out not only what we have done but who we are.

One of the things that struck me during the interviews I conducted for this book was the number of people who came to recognize, either through an employment crisis or otherwise, that their life scripts were being authored by someone else. A man I'll call Norman, for example, who worked in the construction industry for decades before setting out on his own as a photographer, did everything that he was supposed to do, at least according to his family. In high school he played football and was class president and later, after a stint in the military, he followed the admonitions he had received from others which emphasized steadiness, security and achievement.

Those values are fine—even admirable. What was at issue for Norman, however, was the inherited belief that men aren't supposed to be artistic and sensitive—and the fact that he is an artistic, sensitive man.

"When I was a boy it wasn't cool to be an artist or to be sensitive or show your emotions. It took me forty-some years to give myself permission to be able to do that." Norman can now admit that as a boy his sensitivity meant that he sometimes cried—and was severely criticized for it. "I could take a lot of physical abuse but emotionally, if somebody took advantage of me, criticized me, I would cry." Now, he told me, he has learned that it is all right to show emotion and even to cry. It is a lesson that has taken extensive work—not of the paid sort but of the soul sort—attending some seminars on men's issues, participation in a mutual support group, and coming to understand spirituality in a way appropriate for him.

A similar sort of thing was true for Brian, the former university administrator. He recalled his upbringing as emphasizing compliance, a lot of emphasis on "not rocking the boat and being loyal and doing your duty and not arguing. We were not allowed to be angry in our household. We could be sad, but we couldn't be angry. It was preferable to be sad. I think I just picked up a lot of this idea that it was important to get a job, it was important to keep a job, it was important to pay attention to the hierarchy or to the authority in your life. It was important not to get in trouble with the law. Those were basically the recollections that I have."

Although he spent his life as a university administrator, Brian's training was in engineering—which, for various reasons, he chose by a kind of process of elimination. "There was so much about that decision-making process that was just being influenced by other people. There wasn't very much of me in the decision. I knew I was going to university. That was expected. So there was a lot of expert followership and pleasing people, being polite, smiling at the right time, keeping my shoes polished."

Again, there is nothing inherently wrong in those values. The problem is that until recently Brian was not conscious of them and how they had influenced his life. Consequently, he could neither own them nor disown them. As he himself now realizes, his choices were therefore reduced.

Although Brian had begun to work on himself even prior to his employment crisis he remembers the distress associated with being terminated—distress related at least in part to myths he had not yet come to terms with. For example, being in a position which placed him at the center of a lot of attention had been an important component of the job to Brian—which reflected, he feels, a need left over from his upbringing.

As he thought back to getting the letter which effectively ended his job, he said, "I remember this feeling of anger, which I guess came from the fact that I really liked having people pay attention to me and that here was a piece of paper that said, 'Nobody wants to pay attention to you anymore.'

"My father was dead by that time, but it passed through my mind a number of times that if he had been alive, I would have been really mortified, because I wouldn't have been able to explain this. I think he would have been sympathetic, but I would have expected a judgment. You know, you obviously screwed up or this wouldn't have happened, so there was this feeling of humiliation that I shouldn't have gotten myself into this situation.

"So here I was, 22 years into this career, having had the experience of a lot of people being willing to listen to me, and all of a sudden having the tables totally turned on me. Being told not only that I didn't have anything more to say but that they weren't going to listen to what I had been saying, so I might as well buzz off. I guess `betrayed' is the best word to describe how I felt."

Brian's story is obviously filled with pain. But the important thing to note is that he took advantage of the opportunity to grow. He became open to options which he had not previously considered. He has revised his myth, and is now taking a more active part in writing his script.

The same thing has happened for Judith. She is the person,

you may recall, who left a promising career in the healthcare field, took a year off, and subsequently became co-owner of a motorcycle shop. One of the factors involved in her transition was the awareness that she had neglected her nurturing side.

Judith talked a bit about the complex personal mythology that has been hers to process. It includes having "gotten shortchanged on the nurturing side," primarily, she feels, because her mother had grown up in the midst of war and did not learn much about nurturing herself. Judith admitted to being "assertive, even in the early days of my career, fresh out of college. I'd already been introduced to feminists and feminist doctrine, and it was very much part of who I was. Being assertive, aggressive, competitive—I did not consider I was co-opting those things that were traditionally male."

But she also admitted that she played out her role in the corporate world partly to give her father the messages he wanted to hear about her. Telling him that she was leaving that world was therefore not easy. She told her mother of her decision very soon after making it, but several months passed before she told her father.

In her words, "this was going to be one of those moments of `Aha!' revelation, and I was scared I was going to hurt him. But I wasn't going to go through my life hurting *me* more at the expense of not letting my father hear what *he* wanted to hear. That was a critical point in my life, making that split. It was like the umbilical cord of connection with my dad."

While it may not seem that owning a motorcycle shop is a likely outlet for the need to nurture, we should understand that throughout her career much of what Judith regarded as her "real" work had been doing volunteer community service—primarily in connection with AIDS. And, as she explained it to me, her new way of making a living allows her greater freedom for that type of work than had been possible when she was a part of the corporate world. She is writing and living what many would regard as an atypical story. But her words and manner suggested that it is the right one for her.

Since most of the focus of this book is on the development of the self beyond the job work role, most of the stories related here have to do with that struggle. That challenge, I believe, is a very important one for an increasing number of people today. But the specifics will vary considerably from person to person. The common thread is the exploration of what is involved in being "more than" any single role—particularly a role that has been, in effect, assigned to us.

So in some cases developing a fuller sense of identity and self-esteem can mean *choosing* to enter the world of paid work. This is perhaps especially true for young adults. But it can also be true in a broader context. If, for example, a person has been erroneously told that he or she is incapable of holding down a job, or only fits a certain mold, then resisting that imposed limitation can be positive and self-affirming. In that kind of scenario, our real work might well coincide with our job work to a greater extent than usual. In recent times, that situation has been the operative one for an increasing number of women.

Moira, for example, spent more than a decade of her married life playing the role of wife and mother. It was an important role to her, but one that had about it the element of imposition and limitation—just as can be true of the "breadwinner" role for many men. "The messages I had," Moira said as she spoke of her formative years, "were that the prominent thing in your life is being a mother and a wife. Any profession was to be secondary."

But once her sons were well into their school years, Moira resumed the teaching career which she had set aside early in her marriage. And, after several years of teaching, her interests led her into counseling—first as a junior high counselor, then as a career counselor, and later as a guidance counselor. And she was quite articulate in talking about the significance of her career. "It gave me something to be proud of, something which let me feel like I was contributing. It gave me an identity other than mother, which helped to build my self-esteem and let me feel better about myself. I liked being my own person and not just being a wife and mother. I wanted to do something for me."

It is important to note, however, that she also described her self-esteem as having come from some "awfully hard work" she did on herself. That work happened prior to some important career decisions and had to do with confronting the limitations that had been imposed on her by the mythology she had been saddled with growing up.

"I was so caught up in taking care of my mother that even when my boys were small, I would take them with me to take care of her. I was so wrapped up in that, and yet she was so critical of everything I did. I spent time in therapy for about four years, in fact, taking a look at that, and I guess much of my self-esteem came from those four years of working through an awful lot of stuff so I could become my own person.

"I experienced growth. I became proud of that growth and began to see myself as somebody who was capable and whose ideas were OK, who could make a contribution and didn't have to be constantly doing things over like I always did for my Mom. I couldn't even hang the clothes on the line to satisfy her. She'd go and do it over.

"I really became somebody that I could be proud of. I didn't feel proud of me when I was so caught up in her life and her needs. It was difficult to stop that and let her be because I so wanted her to be different. I had to learn that I had no power there, that the power was within me to be who *I* could be."

Moira began to contribute to her own script. And I would argue it was that "work" which made it possible for her to do her paid work so productively and with so much satisfaction. It was that real work which allowed her to move from being a one-dimensional, single identity person. That work was every bit as important as paid work. For Moira, however, it had to be accompanied by paid work. Action was important as well as understanding—which, in different ways for different people, is invariably the case.

"It was after the therapy that I went back to school and got the Education degree. I think my experience in therapy had a bearing on my going into counseling because I felt it had been beneficial to me."

Now retired, Moira recalled that claiming her own identity, listening to her own voice and responding to it with integrity was not always easy—as it seldom is for anyone. That was perhaps especially so when, while teaching and working on her advanced degree, she became pregnant with her third child. In spite of that challenge, however, Moira continued to follow what for her had become a call—not so much to a particular profession as to her own becoming.

Nor has retirement been easy. "For about the first month or two, I wasn't sure I liked it. A year ago I was a high school counselor and I did some private counselling. Today I am Moira, sixty-six years old and retired." But things are starting to change—and it is interesting to note a very significant ingredient that is involved.

"I'm going to be a student," she said, smiling. "I decided to take a course that will be helpful if I decide to go back into counselling. I'm sailing with my husband. I enjoy having time to read. I'm doing jazzercise, which is fun for me and it's been kind of a challenge because I'm older than most of the people in the class. I think there's still room for growth. I don't think people ever reach the ultimate growth. I think you can always keep growing and improving."

What has been true for Moira for much of her adult life and is continuing now is something I'll come back to later as a key factor in the identity developing/becoming process—namely, being a lifelong learner. Continuing to learn contributes greatly to the joy of the journey of identity. And it is worth noting that Moira is taking both the advanced counselling course and her jazzercize class with her married daughter—the now-grown child who was born at what was something of a crossroad in Moira's career development and personal growth.

Earlier, you may remember, I spoke of real work in the framework of a "call"—a call to self-realization. In mythological terms a call is often understood in terms of beginning a new stage of one's journey. It has to do with exploring uncharted, sometimes dangerous territory, not only for the sake of one's own knowledge and understanding, but also for that of the community of which the person taking the journey is a part.

And so it is that we sometimes hear reference to the "hero's journey" or the "heroic quest." That journey or quest takes many forms, but basically it is a rite of passage having three phases: separation, initiation, and return.* It consists, that is, of separation from that which is known; initiation or entry into a new and, in one way or another, dangerous place; and returning with new knowledge, understanding, and strength for the community. The call to make that kind of journey often comes in conjunction with a time of personal vulnerability and uncertainty.

I do not want to get too deeply into ancient mythology here. But we don't have to do so in order to use the hero's journey as a model for speaking imaginatively of an initiation into a deeper level of experience, of the confrontation of challenges rather than the avoidance of them, and of the growth that comes as a result. Likewise, we can view an employment crisis as a "call" to take that kind of journey.

And we need to remember that such a journey—or quest—is really about self-affirmation. As defined succinctly by Carol Pearson in in her book *Awakening the Heroes Within*, "The heroic quest is about saying yes to yourself and, in so doing, becoming more fully alive and more effective in the world."*

Embarking on that journey, however, means that we must go within ourselves—which some people are reluctant to do, mainly because of fear of what they may find. And it is true that there are some dangers and risks involved—just as there always are when we go into territory that is unknown. But to refuse to take those risks, to refuse to know ourselves in depth, is to refuse to discover who we really are.

It is not only to refuse to confront those parts of ourselves that may be disconcerting, but it is also to fail to open the way to strengths and resources we may have neglected or not known. To refuse to know ourselves is to give our identity over to others—often to the cultural average, the lowest possible denominator.

One of the things involved in exploring our inner life in depth is what is known as "the shadow" in human experience. The shadow, a term most often associated with the psychotherapist Carl Jung, consists of those parts of ourselves that we do not want to acknowledge.* One way to imagine it is as a bag full of secrets that we drag along behind us.

Sometimes we think of the shadow as containing only the "negative" parts of ourselves—our anger, our jealousies, perhaps our sexual fantasies. But as the concept of the shadow has evolved, it has come to be understood as including all of those parts of ourselves that we deny, that we neglect, that we don't want to acknowledge. As such, it can include positive qualities which we have been conditioned to believe are somehow not quite "respectable." An example which immediately comes to mind is Norman, the man who left the construction industry to become a photographer and who for most of his life relegated his sensitivity and creativity to the realm of his shadow.

Our shadow begins to develop in childhood and is essentially a response to early conditioning. If we are told or sense from the reactions of the adults who care for us that certain behavior is disapproved of, we "stuff" it into our shadow bag. As we grow and mature, of course, most of us learn to let some things out of that bag.

We may have been taught, for example, that it's bad to be selfish with one's toys. As we mature, however, we come to understand that it's appropriate to be selfish in some situations, such as refusing to let a roommate borrow a blouse or a shirt because it's the one you want to wear that evening.

If we fail to do that kind of learning, we are likely to suffer as a result. We may, for example, believe that we aren't entitled to take time for ourselves and so we give all of it to "the company," only to suffer health problems and an identity crisis at the loss of our job, as Leon did.

The problem is really twofold. For one thing, it takes a lot of energy to keep all of our shadow parts stuffed in a bag. So some of them invariably get out and show themselves in ways that are inappropriate—for example, we may throw a temper tantrum over something quite inconsequential. And the other part of the problem is that we lose a lot of our strength and creativity by keeping those parts tucked away. We deny parts of ourselves which, if acknowledged, can be incorporated into who we are in a beneficial way.

Reclaiming our shadow parts is not a matter of "acting out." In fact, acting out is often a symptom of *not* having acknowledged all parts of ourselves. Instead, we can claim and use the energy that resides in the shadow for our own benefit. Rather than "exploding" over something, for example, we can learn, by acknowledging our anger, to assert ourselves appropriately in pursuit of the things we want. To know and to embrace one's shadow is to know oneself as a whole person, not as one divided between good and bad, weakness and strength, positive and negative.

One misguided way in which we often try to deal with the shadow is by what is known as "projection." That is, we project onto other people those parts of ourselves which we neglect or want to deny. In some cases our projection is accompanied by anger. We may, for example, be very critical of people who seem to be lazy—which may in fact be a sign that we haven't come to terms with our own need to relax from time to time.

But the other side of the coin, emphasized by Jungian therapist Robert Johnson in his book *Owning Your Own Shadow,* is that our shadow is also revealed when we project the *best* of ourselves onto others.* We do that sort of thing, for example, when we idolize others—for their creativity, ingenuity, courage, or some other quality—and insist that we don't have those qualities within ourselves. To be overawed by what we perceive as another person's ability and value is sign that we are failing to honor our own value and abilities.

The tendency of most of us is to resist even becoming aware of our shadow side, much less taking the time and energy required to engage it and find creative ways to derive strength and power from it. But doing so is a major part of what our real work is about—getting to know ourselves fully, not as an exercise in self-indulgence, but for the sake of being able to live out our lives creatively and caringly.

To come to terms with our shadow is a major part of that endeavor. It is to discover that an "either/or" view of ourselves is inadequate and instead to embrace a "both/and" perspective. We thus learn to view ourselves—and to embrace ourselves—as whole persons rather than divided ones. And we discover, in the words of Robert Johnson, that "our fate can truly be altered if we have the courage to embrace the opposites."*

There is no set formula for knowing yourself. But the one thing that is crucial is honesty. This involves going within and getting in touch with your multidimensional self, including your shadow. It has to do with acknowledging what is important to you, what is valuable in you, and therefore what is worth struggling for. The corollary is that it means giving yourself permission to pursue responsibly those things which you value. The endeavor requires courage, but it can be transformative.

A caveat, however, must be included here. Some people's stories include exceedingly painful memories, some of them buried very deep. If you are one of those people, you need not feel apologetic. But you may want to proceed with caution in reviewing some parts of your story. You may want to have someone trustworthy with whom you can talk about the experience—preferably someone who knows something about venturing into territory of that sort. In fact, that suggestion—to have a supportive person available as you make the journey of self-discovery—is a sound idea for anyone.

There are at least two ways of approaching your story. One is to use the story form itself—to write an autobiography. The other is to view your life using the image of a map. In a sense, both approaches are the same. For an autobiography can be thought of as a kind of journal in retrospect. And a journal is, quite literally, a record of a journey. To be more specific, it is a record of *each day* of a journey.

The important thing is that you do some kind of written record of your life story. One of the things we often overlook is the value of writing. It is not quite the same as talking with a trusted friend or group of friends. But it can help you see yourself more clearly, often with a sense of greater affirmation. So do it as a gift to yourself. And keep in mind that it does not have to be limited to writing. You may, for example, wish to include some drawings. Remember that it's for you; no one else has to see it.

Whatever format you choose for recording your story, I urge you to pay as little attention as possible to your employment history, or to work done as part of the role you see as being your main social identity. At times, of course, information about your job work history will overlap or coincide with the story of yourself as a whole. But the focus here is not on job work; the focus is on the story of yourself beyond the workplace— beyond what you have been led to believe is your primary identity.

With those things things in mind, I want to try to help you think about your story by raising some topics you might want to consider. They are certainly not the only ones possible; in fact, I hope that they will suggest others to you and that you will add to the "assignment," as it were, as you go along. But maybe I can help get you going.

The thing to remember is the main question: *Who are you?*

If you begin by sketching something that might look like a roadmap, you will likely discover that it takes the form of a combination of straight highways and side roads. Think about which have been more typical for you. Consider what the side roads represent. Do they suggest parts of yourself that you've wanted to explore further but haven't allowed yourself to? Have the side roads been more interesting than the main highways?

Some people are more achievement oriented while others are more inclined toward exploration. The achievers are the ones who want to go to the top of the mountain as quickly as possible. They are the ones our culture rewards and approves of most readily. Many people—men in particular—spend their lives trying to fit that model even when it isn't right for them at all.

But there are also the explorers. They—and I include myself among them—want to take side trips, want to explore the mountain on the way up. We may think of "the heroic" as being the exclusive province of achievers. But it can also apply to the journeys of those who are more inclined to take time for exploration.

As you look over your roadmap and start to make a few notations here and there, take time to think a little bit about the messages you got from your family of origin. What values and priorities were communicated to you as you grew up? What expectations were placed upon you? What expectations did you place upon yourself? Who were your role models? What were you told about your strengths, about your limitations, about what was important in life?

Remember that the messages that we get do not always come to us directly. Often it's more the case that we "absorb" what is important about how life should be lived. The messages, moreover, are usually mixed. And how we respond to them, how we "dialogue" with them is determined by a myriad of factors.

In my own case, I grew up knowing certain things about my parents, about the families they came from, and about the values encoded in those stories. My father was the youngest son in a family of eleven. From their humble beginnings in the southern part of the United States, he and his brothers and sisters scattered and settled from California to New York.

I never felt that I knew my father's side of the family very well. One of his brothers lived in the city where I grew up, but they had little in common. Dad was a self-made businessman, involved from time to time in civic affairs; my uncle had little ambition. Our families got together from time to time, but the bond was not a close one.

In contrast, my mother's side of the family, the Sheffields, were closer to each other. None of my mother's brothers and sisters lived in our city. But it always seemed that they kept in reasonably close touch and that, while there was some family bickering, there was a good deal of warmth between them when they were together. Family reunions were valued by the Sheffields. As far as I can remember, the Harrisons never considered an event of that sort.

I never knew either of my grandfathers. But as I grew up I learned that my grandfather Harrison was a farmer—an easygoing man, apparently, but one upon whom fortune did not shine. He died when my father was in his teens, leaving my grandmother with a large family to raise and virtually no resources other than her own tenacity—which was considerable. On the other side, Grandfather Sheffield farmed, raised cattle, and had a meat market. He was certainly not well-to-do, but he was apparently a pillar of church and community and an adequate provider.

We are told that birth order has a lot to do with the way in which children adapt. In my case I was first, middle, and last—in other words, an only child. It was not supposed to have been that way—at least not in my father's scheme of things. But my mother's poor health and a difficult pregnancy meant that his hopes for a large family had to be altered.

I grew up aware of that fact and of some parts of their stories, their identities. For Mother that included religion (Southern Baptist) and books (she had been a teacher before her marriage). For Dad it included many of the traits of self-made men: pride, strong opinions, and a commitment to hard work. (And at mother's urging he did become involved in church life.) Mother was also known for her caregiving and for the knitting she did; one of Dad's "trademarks" was his laugh, which could be heard across quite a large room.

Growing up, I was told that I should choose an occupation I would enjoy. But I also think I sensed what the hoped for agendas were. For Mother it was that I should be a minister—which I pursued as a course of study for a time. And if Dad had had his "druthers," I would have been an engineer and a businessman, with a stint as a professional baseball player thrown in. But I would be remiss if I did not emphasize that both of them were always encouraging of my career choices.

From both of my parents I learned the value of determination in the face of adversity. For Dad, adversity was mainly economic. After coming out of service in the First World War, he spent more than a decade working as a carpenter, first in one place and then another, apparently never losing a determination to "make something of himself." To him that notion meant more than making a living, but it definitely included being self-employed. And he finally started to realize that dream around the time he turned 40—around the time he and my mother married and about a year before I was born.

Mother too knew about economic adversity. During the Great Depression she had been paid for her teaching with vouchers. And one story I heard a number of times was that she and my father had less than $50.00 between them when they married in 1935.

But for Mother adversity also took the form of poor health—which started to plague her early in her marriage and continued throughout the rest of her life. But her strength was greater than some thought. I remember hearing that shortly after I was born she was told her that she would be lucky to live to see me graduate from high school. I was fifty-three when she died.

Of course I could go on. But my intention is not to go into laborious detail about the messages that I have received, struggled with, revised, and, in some cases, rejected. It is, rather, to try to illustrate that we are all repositories of a set of myths—a complicated, sometimes contradictory way of understanding the world—which has its roots not only in our own experience but also the histories of our families and communities.

That mythology is in a continuing process of unfolding. Throughout our lives we peel away layers and we add layers. It is an ongoing combination of unlearning and learning, of letting go of that which is old and unworkable and claiming that which gives meaning and significance to our lives.

Having encouraged you to think about your own mythology and the stories you grew up hearing, let me go on to suggest that you consider some of the ways in which they have affected your life—your feelings about job work and its importance, yes, but also your feelings about making a life, about the larger meaning of success and failure. Remember that this is about more than your job work self or its equivalent, though you should not be surprised if you find that your attention keeps shifting back to that limited focus, as if by default.

Then move on to think about the labels that might describe you. You may well be conscious of the one called "breadwinner" and the importance you have attached to it. But take a few minutes to reflect on some of the others. Think about words that you might use to describe yourself, and about those that others might use to describe you. Your friends, for example. Members of your family. Your neighbors. The people you work with, or have worked with. Give some thought to how you are different in different settings.

We present different "fronts" to different people. Which is as it should be. You probably wouldn't want a boss to know everything about you that your spouse, lover, or closest friend does. But it can be instructive to give some thought to the differences between our private selves and our public ones.

The idea, remember, is to ask yourself *"who am I?"*—and to push really hard for the answers. Imagine introducing yourself to a stranger without referring to your work or to any other standardized label. Use the phrase *I am* and follow it with a short phrase that names a characteristic or a trait that you consider true of yourself. And give yourself some latitude. Think of things about yourself that you have often dismissed as unimportant—things like the pleasure you take in singing in the shower or growing roses. Be imaginative.

As you think about the labels and traits and characteristics which help to define you, consider which ones would be hardest to give up. Leave job work off the list and focus on the others—public and private. What would be left if all of the defining elements in your life were taken away? *Who* would be left? Can you think of ways of defining yourself that could *not* be taken away, short of taking away your life?

What is the quality of your relationships with the people significant to you? How much time and attention have you given to the people you care about deeply? Many of the individuals I talked with have come to place more importance on their close relationships as a result of getting to know themselves better. They have discovered a fundamental truth: we shortchange ourselves if we fail to nurture the supportive relationships we may have.

How about the pace of your life? On a scale of one to ten, rate how rushed you feel. How satisfying is it to live at the pace you do? What are you running from? What are you running toward? What do you hope to escape, to find, or to achieve by living at your present pace?

Sometimes the harder we try to fill the empty spaces in our lives, the deeper they get. We can learn a great deal about ourselves by listening to what goes on inside us when we slow down and allow ourselves to experience solitude. For some people there's a sense of relief. For others, however, it is very frightening.

Take some time to reflect on the things that move you, that evoke in you feelings of wonder and awe. They might include looking into the eyes of a loved one, seeing trust reflected on a child's face, gazing at the stars on a clear night or at a blade of grass in the early morning dew, listening to a particular piece of music, reading a poem, or standing before a painting or other work of art. What we feel at such times is an important part of who we are. But it has nothing to do with what we are paid to do.

Remember the things that have made you feel good about yourself—things you have done that have been affirming for you. Think about your victories—the times when you stood up for yourself, when you did something that was difficult for you, when you achieved what you set out to achieve. Give yourself credit for those things. Give some thought to the parts of yourself that are reflected in those happenings.

Think about your issues—the concerns that you've struggled with repeatedly over your life. Maybe they have to do with the search for approval, or with rebellion. Perhaps you have persistently felt rootless or in a rut. Maybe you've repeatedly wanted to venture onto new paths, more creative than the ones you've stuck with, but haven't been able to make that move. Or maybe you've been prone to think that "the grass is always greener" somewhere other than where you are. Whatever your issues are, think about how you have dealt with them—or not dealt with them. Have you run from them or confronted them? Do they need further "work?"

What interests have fallen by the wayside on your journey? Maybe there are things you didn't exactly *drop* along the way—or didn't intend to—but you set them aside. What are some of the things you keep saying you are going to do once you finish the ones you are *supposed* to do? Most of us have things we've always been going to do—tomorrow. And we often fail to do them, at least in part because of the myth common to our culture which says that only the "practical" matters, that only the objectives with financial value are worth making into priorities.

But some people do manage to pursue them—even if they do so belatedly. I recently heard, for example, about a woman who had always wanted to take tap dancing lessons. Which she did—following her retirement. She even participated in a dance recital, along with much younger people. More power to her!

So think about the things that energize you—things which

you do because you want to rather than because you have to, things you do for love rather than for money. Such things provide us with what psychologists sometimes call "peak experiences" or "optimal experiences." They are the activities in which we at once "lose ourselves" and "find ourselves." Unfortunately, these are the things we too often say we'll do tomorrow.

What have been some of the turning points in your life—the times when you made a major decision but might have made another? Can you remember the issues involved at those points? Was fear an important player? The need to prove something to yourself or someone else? Wanting to please someone else? Not wanting to rock the boat? Think about some of the things you have learned as a result of one or more of those decisions.

Remember that there's no point in asking whether or not we would make the same decision again. We were operating with the only information we had at the time. But what do you know now—especially about yourself—that you did not know then? What might you *not* have learned about yourself if you had made the "other" decision? Keep in mind that the object isn't to stir up regret; it is not to castigate ourselves for the decisions we have made. The object is simply to look at some of those decisions in retrospect in order to see if we can learn more about who we are.

In his book *Transitions,* William Bridges suggests that we need to reflect on our story, perhaps especially when we are in the midst of change or contemplating change, because the *past keeps changing*. It's true: from the standpoint of a new present, the past looks different. The past, Bridges argues, "isn't like a landscape or a vase of flowers that is just *there*. It is more like the raw material awaiting a builder."*

Which brings us to the question: what is it that you are searching for? What do you want out of life? Think about the future—and your hopes for it. Are you searching for a place to be comfortable, where you can feel secure and complacent? Or can you envisage a future which allows for unfolding, for surprises?

How would you occupy your time if you no longer had to work or look for work?

If, in doing this review, you find contradictions in yourself, don't be disturbed. That's as it should be. It is neither possible nor desirable for all parts of ourselves to fit together with perfect consistency. Wholeness, as I use the word, can accommodate creative tension between various parts of ourselves. It can accommodate the fact that we are defined, at least in part, by our contradictions. The object is not to eliminate the contradictions, but to know them honestly and work with them imaginatively.

And remember that self-knowledge is never complete. As St. Paul reminds us in his first letter to the Corinthians, we see "through a glass darkly" and know ourselves only "in part." But our identity is found by continuing to explore and confront those facts of our lives which we perceive but dimly. And so the object in doing this review is to see if there are parts of ourselves which may have gotten lost in the shuffle or left by the wayside. Almost invariably, most of us find, there are.

I'm not suggesting that we can do everything we've always wanted to do—or that we should try. But sometimes a crisis—such as one involving employment—can remind us of what we have left along the way. In some cases we may be able to do some retrieving. But even if we can't, the remembering itself can be important.

We are sometimes led to believe that our growth and development are supposed to end once we reach a certain age or finish school. But to accept that idea is to try to fix our identity rather than understand it as a journey. It continues to unfold—or should continue to unfold—throughout our lives. And the "work" associated with it has many faces, not all of which have anything to do with pay.

By being aware of your story, you have a better grasp of what is important to you. You are therefore free to double back, as it were, and pay attention to things that may have been neglected earlier. The hero's journey—the journey of self-discovery and self-actualization—is neither linear nor circular. It is more like a spiral. We keep going around at ever deepening levels, interacting and creating as we go, transforming our circumstances and being transformed by them, getting in touch with and affirming those parts of our self that are more than any label.

Sam's story is another one which illustrates the importance of learning to know oneself. A senior executive for much of his career life, Sam admitted, "I wanted prestige, and of course the more money I had the more I felt that we should have the bigger station wagon, that we should send the kids to music lessons, that we should have all the things we're taught to want. I believed the values that men are taught—that they have to provide."

Sam also wanted to become the national director of one of the divisions of his company. But when the opportunity came, he realized, "I didn't want it. I had come to feel that the job had taken total control of me, and I was leaving *me* somewhere behind." As one of two finalists for the position, he decided to withdraw and to take early retirement.

He attributes the change in large part to his wife, who, he said, "feels that you have to live the total of life. She made me face and deal with a lot of the things that I had been denying or sweeping under the carpet.

"I found that to have the kind of success I was looking for you must have power. And to achieve power, trust goes out the window. You have to throw away the qualities that make life full, and our corporate structure teaches us to do that."

He spoke movingly and from experience of career-oriented people who have a way of saying things to their children like, "Well, what you need can wait because this crap I brought home in my briefcase has to be looked at. So walk for awhile if your bicycle's broken. I've got this work to do. I'll fix it later."

Sam's transition did not happen overnight. It was spread over ten years and the greatest revelation came, at least in part, because of a heart attack. Sam took time off from work, went back again, and then, after a backpacking trip in Europe (which his doctor didn't want him to take) he agreed to tests which revealed arterial blockage and the need for open heart surgery. After the surgery, "I was off work for more than two hundred days. And I decided I didn't want to go back, so I took medical retirement. But for more than ten years, since I met and subsequently married my second wife, I had been changing my feeling about work."

Still, leaving the world of regular job work was a challenge. "I used to walk into a social gathering having one of the most senior management positions in my part of the country and all kinds of doors and conversations opened to me. Now I better understand how unemployed individuals feel about people asking, `What do you do?' That's the first question in a social setting, `What do you do for a living?' `Well, I'm retired,' `Oh,' they say, and they walk away."

Sam said he has learned to view that kind of behavior as other people's problem and, "as far as filling the gaps of self-worth, you do other things to satisfy your need, because people have a need to be needed. What most of us do is fill that need to be needed with a job. That's what I did, but I had to change. I had to look at different ways to satisfy my need to be needed."

Sam went on to talk more about the fact that the transition hasn't been easy. "For the longest time, even as I climbed the corporate ladder, I was pissed off with myself. I guess I had thought there should be something more, but I didn't know what. So I substituted getting more things, getting a better job in order to buy more, getting more recognition. I feel I've missed a lot of years getting to where I am now, but other people who are still doing what I did would probably say I'm wasting time, letting all my great success go to crap."

Now Sam finds success in other ways. "My wife runs her own business and I do some research for her, preparing training manuals and other things. And I putter around in my garden. I also work with people in various ways. For instance, I've always been a pretty good handyman. And so people doing home renovations often call me up and say things like, `Look, I want to wire my recreation room, will you do it for me?' And I say, `No, but I'll show you how to do it so when I'm not around you can still do it.' So I'll go over and show them how to do the work and help them do it, and there's a big payoff in that for me."

As Sam's case illustrates, the object of getting in touch with your story is not to deny the importance of any type of employment. It is rather to put employment in the perspective of your own choosing, one which allows for the development of the person who is distinctly you. As noted earlier, all of us are made up of many dimensions. It is to remember that we have many needs, many interests, and many labels. We need to give attention to all of them. We need to concern ourselves with making a life as well as making a living.

In doing so we may find that we prefer to spend more time on things that matter to us and less on those that matter to someone else's bottom line. We may find that we prefer—and have the option of choosing—a life that is hand tailored rather than ready made. We may discover that we can make our lives into distinctive works of art.

In each of us there is what is known as "entelechy"—which is more or less synonymous with "potential." One way of understanding entelechy is that it is the unique form of an oak tree encoded in an acorn. In broader terms, it is about the sum of the possibilities and potentialities encoded in any living entity, including individual human beings. It is the unique potential encoded in each of us.

Our real work is to nourish our entelechy—our potential. And we do so by attending not to just one part of ourselves but to our *selves* as a whole. We have met some people who are pursuing that kind of self-realization. In the pages ahead we will meet others. And we will discuss some of the stances toward living which can encourage that process.

Part of realizing our potential, ironically, is claiming and honoring our woundedness, our vulnerability, and our shadow. That statement is not by any means a call to self-pity or to identify ourselves as victims. It has to do, rather, with the recognition that woundedness is an inevitable part of growth and maturity. Our woundedness is linked with our struggles, which in turn have to do with the things we care deeply about. We don't get to be fully human without being wounded.

Ours is a culture, however, which emphasizes wound-free living—or at least the illusion of wound-free living. But our wounds are the ways in which the sacred, the most significant, and the most authentic enter into human life. It is by embracing ourselves in our totality—warts and all, as the saying goes—that we are transformed, that we find new power and strength.

Let me try to illustrate this idea further by introducing you to Frank. Like many of the people I talked with, Frank had followed the work prescription laid down for him by his family. Almost immediately, however, things started to unfold in a way that didn't really follow the "script." For example, after getting a college degree, he discovered that the only job he could find was manual work in a gravel pit. "Which," he noted with irony, "is what I'd been told all through high school I'd wind up doing if I didn't get my diploma."

After three years of this type of work he returned to school, got his teaching certificate, and succeeded in finding a job as an elementary teacher. Seven years later, however, he had a nervous breakdown, related in large part to his trying to live up to other people's expectations in his work and elsewhere. He then took a leave of absence and entered therapy.

"I was totally disillusioned," he recalled. "I thought I'd always be a school teacher. I thought I'd found my niche and it was just going to go on." But during the course of his leave he also realized that a number of other things were going on within him and that he did not want to return to teaching. This realization was very difficult for Frank: "My training had all led to being a teacher, and I just felt that I was washed up because it was the only kind of work I was qualified for. I had lost the vision for my life. I guess I really did identify my self with what I did. That was my identity, and I had lost it.

"I was unemployed. I went through a tremendous loss of self-esteem when I couldn't find work. I didn't feel a sense of worth. I was the father of four children, and had been married for about fifteen years. It seemed there wasn't a place for me to explore whatever my gifts or talents were."

To help support his family, Frank took over a job a friend had vacated as a truck driver. His route took him onto the campus of a major university. And, he recalled, "every time I went there, every Thursday, I had this incredible sense of serenity. I felt like I was coming home. One thing led to another and I applied and was accepted in the Adult Education Department. But right next door was Counseling Psychology. I knew I was in some process of looking for the next step in my career, and I finally sensed it would be in counseling."

Perhaps even more significant for Frank was a dream he had. "It was when I was thirty-eight and just before I started to go back to school. In the dream I was ascending a mountain and rather than doing switchbacks to go up the mountainside or going around the mountain in a kind of spiral, I was walking more or less straight up one side of it. I was kicking a ball somewhat like a rugby ball. But it was an odd shape, and it wouldn't bounce straight ahead, and I would have to go and search to find it. It was getting dark and I would lose it and then find it.

"But finally," he went on, "I held this odd ball next to my bosom and it became part of me. And to my understanding, the dream was that once I accepted my uniqueness, my `oddballness' as it were, I could continue my ascent to wherever I was going. By the time I reached the summit of the mountain, it was pitch dark, absolute night, except that the sky was filled with stars, and as I lifted up my hands in wonder, I actually began to ascend into the stars."

Frank feels that embracing his "oddballness" has helped to

empower him to make the sacrifices necessary to become a practicing psychotherapist. But he spoke of his job work as being "more of a mission than an identity. In my first professional job, as a teacher, I looked to the professional identity, the degree behind my name as part of who I was. It was after I lost that external sense of identity that I found an internal source of identity in becoming the person I am.

"I feel my identity is now rooted in who I am rather than what I do for a living. And there's a greater comfort zone for me because who I am is apparent as a psychologist, as a friend, as a backpacker—it's just me. It's OK to be just me and there's no one else like me."

I don't know exactly what Frank considers his "oddballness," but it really doesn't matter. For we all have some part of ourselves which we feel is a little bit odd—some part of our story, our character, which doesn't seem to us to fit the "norm." Nor does it matter that Frank's embrace of that part of himself was made possible by a dream. What is important is not the particulars of his experience, but the essential part of it. What is important is that he moved to a level of self-understanding and affirmation which embraced his whole person.

One of the stories that comes to us from ancient Greece has to do with what is known as the Procrustean Bed. The story tells of how travelers on their way to Athens were caught by a figure named Procrustes, placed in a bed of his, and made to fit. If they were too short, they were stretched; if they were too long, their size was reduced. And according to Jean Shinoda Bolen, writing in her book *Gods in Everyman,* to be "on the way to Athens" was a kind of metaphor for those committed to success and all its trappings.*

It seems to me our most common notion of identity can be a kind of Procrustean Bed—which is to say it can insist that our identity is based primarily on what we do for a living. By doing so it emphasizes identity as "fixed" and one-dimensional and self-esteem as being tied to that identity.

Some people, of course, are content to be defined in that way. But many, including some of the most gifted and creative, are not. And thus we are back to the legacy from ancient Greece with which I began this chapter: Know yourself.

It may seem strange to juxtapose the recommendation to know yourself with the story of the Procrustes and his bed. But we cannot escape the struggle implicit in that juxtaposition. For if we are to know ourselves in depth, we must find the courage to insist that our deepest self is violated by having it boxed up in some nice, neat, commercial package, and then being led to believe that the work is over and done with once that packaging is complete.

To be sure, part of the socialization process we all go through involves learning to "fit in." I am not arguing for anarchy, or for any kind of behavior that is damaging to oneself or others. But to take those fitted parts as the sum total of our identity is to do ourselves a disservice. For the sake of our wholeness, therefore, we need to try to discover or recover those parts of ourselves that may have gotten lost along the way.

The object, however, is not to replace one fixed identity with another one, although we may change our primary mask from, say, salesman to househusband or from mother to real estate agent. The main object of moving beyond a sense of self as little or nothing more than our assigned social role is to discover a different dimension of living, a different view of working. As philosopher Sam Keen expresses it in his book *The Passionate Life,* "to love the self is not to come upon an unchangeable image or essence, but to welcome all the diversity of experience into consciousness."*

The object, moreover, is not self-indulgence; it is not for the sake of living for ourselves alone. It is, rather, to affirm ourselves as persons at once whole and filled with contradictions, to become open to *being* as well as to *knowing,* and to participate in and celebrate the richness of life. It is to use our gifts and strengths for others as well as for ourselves. It is to respond creatively to life—which will be the focus of our next chapter.

Chapter Four

THE PATH OF CREATIVE RESPONSE

Our most authentic sense of identity and self-esteem comes not so much from what happens to us as from how we respond to the circumstances with which we are confronted. To be human is to be responsible—to be *able* to respond. And living responsibly means responding to things as they are, even when they are not what we would like them to be.

Much of our responding is done routinely and with little thought, more or less as if we were sleepwalking. But a different kind of response is possible, one which draws upon our creativity. That kind of response invites us to see ourselves and our circumstances in a perspective that can be fresh and empowering.

The common notion of creativity is that it is the province of a select few—artists, musicians, poets, playwrights, and novelists. Or, to expand that kind of view a little, it is understood as something that has to do with brainstorming, a way of pulling a solution out of a hat when ordinary approaches come up short.

By that definition, creativity is thought of as being exercised in conjunction with talents or skills which facilitate the production or interpretation of a specific entity—a musical composition, a work of art, a piece of writing, or a business plan or advertising campaign. And, all too often, we break the combination of talent and creativity into two categories—that which involves remuneration, and that which does not. The former, we tend to think, is somehow more important than the latter. In either case, creativity is thought of as the province of a select few and in terms of end results or products.

I do not want to disparage any exercise of creativity. On the contrary, I think poetry, art, and music are too important to leave to the professionals. They have enormous potential for our well-being—a point I'll come back to later in the book. And there is no doubt but that creativity is often seen in any number of occupations. But for now I want to point out that creativity can also be understood in another way—not unrelated to the first, but distinct from it.

What I am talking about is what the psychologist Abraham Maslow termed "self-actualizing creativity."* It is an inner resource which allows for *living* creatively, to the fullest of one's potential. Which means that people can be creative even if they do not work in any of the environments usually associated with creativity or produce any of the objects or accomplishments often thought of in connection with it.

Seen in this light, creativity has more to do with process and with one's journey than with a particular product or destination. It has to do with opening oneself to a rich and deep source of energy—which can be of benefit both in making a living and in making a life.

To draw upon that resource is to align ourselves with the creative process that is part of all of nature. Doing so allows us to live with integrity, authenticity, and an appropriate sense of control—which is important to self-esteem and dignity. We are better able to deal with and learn from life's crises, including those having to do with employment.

To respond to life creatively is to make use of what we have, to refashion it in different and imaginative ways which allow us to find meaning, connection, and a true sense of who we are. It involves improvisation and incorporates trust, faith, and courage. It may have to do with making a living. It invariably has to do with the art of living, which Jungian therapist Frances Wickes, author of *The Inner World of Choice,* has described as being "of all creative arts the most difficult and the most distinguished."*

Often, when confronted with a challenge, we may feel that we are faced with the choice of reacting passively or aggressively, of being a victim or a warrior, of either fighting or fleeing. Responding creatively offers a middle ground between those two kinds of extremes. What it involves, in effect, is the ability to work with circumstances, with the way in which life is unfolding. Rather than being reactive or proactive, it calls for being interactive. To be interactive is to work as diligently and creatively as possible to find a solution to the challenges confronting us, while at the same time trusting that we can make valuable discoveries about ourselves in the process.

To be interactive is, on a personal level, to bring into being. But that stance avoids the notion that one is totally responsible for the way in which his or her life unfolds. It accepts, rather, a sharing of responsibility. We may not have a choice in all of the circumstances which confront us. In fact, we seldom do. But we do have choices in how we respond. And the act of making those choices will contribute to our dignity, self-esteem, and sense of identity if we let it.

It seems to me not unlike a truth related to art—and, for that matter, to all of life. For there is a sense in which a work of art only becomes a work of art through a person's response. Until we respond to it, a painting by Van Gogh, Reubens, Picasso, Rockwell, or any other artist is simply a combination of colors or lines on a canvas. It "becomes" art as we interact with it. And the same thing is true of music, of poetry, of drama—and, for that matter, of human relationships.

Of course, the "becoming" may take awhile. I may not "get" a poem the first time I read it, or a joke the first time I hear it. But by opening myself to whatever reality is there, I do my part to bring that reality into being. What that means in a larger sense is that by responding creatively we literally *co-create the world in which we live.*

To respond creatively is to engage with life—not in the sense of trying to pound it into submission but in the sense of being open to it, of interacting with it. And unless we engage with life, we are only half alive. In the oft-quoted words of Helen Keller, "life is either a daring adventure or nothing."*

Creativity is directly related to soul and spirit as well as to our workaday identity. It requires courage, faith, risk-taking, and patience. It is at the heart of our becoming. It makes it possible for us to honor the questions of life—and, in the process, to move toward answers and understanding. It is crucial to our getting free of our fixed, one-dimensional, job-based identity.

It would be nice if I could list three or four or seven steps to living more creatively. Unfortunately, however, it is not that simple—at least not in my view. But the starting point is that we destroy judgment—or at least suspend judgment. We have to accept that things may not always be the way they seem, that the standard way of doing things is not the only way, and that there are discoveries about ourselves which we have yet to make.

We also have to learn to turn off or tune out our "inner voice of doubt." Everyone has some form of that voice. It's the one which says things like, "you could never get a job that good," "you're not a writer," "what makes you think you've got any good ideas?" or "you haven't got what it takes to be in business for yourself." The variations are endless—if we let them be. But we can learn to recognize them for what they are and can discover that we don't have to listen to them.

One thing that has helped me has been to become aware of when my inner voice of doubt is the strongest. Which, for me, is late in the afternoon. So I've learned that after about 5:00 p.m., I should try especially hard to ignore any inner messages I may hear about my abilities—or lack thereof. And having found I can downplay them then, I've become a little better able to do it at other times.

In addition to quieting our inner doubts—the corollary of which is staying curious and keeping an open mind—we can foster creativity by becoming aware of some of its attributes. By doing so I believe we can discover—or at least catch a glimpse of—patterns which can help us deal with the challenges of living and assist us in getting in touch with the most authentic parts of ourselves.

By its very nature, creativity is heuristic. That is, it unfolds without a set of fixed rules. Which may give some of us trouble, for we like to believe in orderly processes. We like to plan ahead. We like to think that "A" is followed by "B" which is followed by "C," and that if we do certain things, certain other things will follow. One example is the belief that if we work hard we will be rewarded. This can be true, but our rewards can take many different forms.

One thing we should remember in talking about the heuristic nature of creativity is that the root of the word heuristic is the same root from which we get the word (and exclamation) "Eureka!" By that term, we refer to the moments when insight comes seemingly from out of the blue, when a lightbulb suddenly seems to come on in our mind. Which is a further reminder that creativity has a life of its own and operates by "rules" which are different from ordinary ones. We cannot plan moments of insight. We cannot be sure exactly how things will turn out.

That fact is a constant for anyone involved in any kind of creative endeavor—whether it be writing a book, crafting a piece of pottery, or starting a business. For in the act of creation, the object of creation invariably takes on a "life" of its own. And while there is much to be said for trying to keep projects on "course," there is evidence to suggest that works of art begun without a fixed expectation as to how they should turn out may in fact be the ones with the greatest artistic merit.*

At the risk of sounding frivolous, it is also the case that life itself takes on a "life" of its own. Life is what happens while we are making plans and working toward goals. But given the understanding of creativity I am suggesting, those truths do not have to be all negative.

This is not to argue that goals are unimportant, but it is to suggest that we can shortchange ourselves by being obsessed with them. Expectations and projected outcomes need to be kept in perspective. Living mainly for the future—which most of us are programmed to do—is to do ourselves a disfavor. The nature of creativity, it seems to me, reminds us of these things. Having said them, however, I must go on to say that there *is* a kind of orderliness to the creative realm—at least if we understand that it is connected with the natural world. There is a certain dependability about the way in which things unfold in that world. Day does follow night. The cycle of the seasons does repeat, and spring does follow winter.

Part of the natural world's dependability has to do with the cycle of death and rebirth, of disintegration and reintegration, of the old breaking down and the new emerging. Things sometimes have to break down in order to come back together again. Some times we have to lose to gain. Sometimes parts of us have to "die" so that we may become more fully alive.

The truths that are implicit in the natural world are affirmed by spiritual traditions throughout the world. As the late mythologist Joseph Campbell pointed out, the truly religious rites and ceremonies of all cultures are designed to help people accept those kinds of truths; there have never been rites to keep winter from coming.*

There is, to be sure, a time not to change. But there is also a time for changing. Therefore, to be consistently overattached to any part of one's life—including, I suggest, one's job work identity—is to resist the truth implicit in the realm of creativity.

But it is possible to trust in the creative process, to pursue goals and dreams in a way that reflects our connection to it. We can learn to embrace the creative process and find strength in the dynamic involved in it. To do so can help us respond with hope and courage to life's ebb and flow: the disappointments, the small deaths, as it were, the losses which can be painful but which are nevertheless an integral part of our growth and development.

To try to avoid those realities, to think that we are immune to them, is to try to deny our humanity. Sometimes a crisis of employment will bring that truth home in such a way that we become open to a deeper understanding of who we are. It can move us toward saying yes to life, even in the midst of our grieving times.

At the same time, however, we are invited to act, to dialogue with our circumstances, to experiment. We are invited to *improvise*—which philosopher Stephen Nachmanovitch, author of the book *Free Play,* calls "a master key to creativity.* And thus we are drawn to a part of the creative realm which will be clearly recognizable to us.

For we all improvise. When we see a traffic jam up ahead, we take an alternate route. If we don't have the romaine lettuce called for by the recipe, we use leaf lettuce instead. If we find we can't keep an appointment, we reschedule. Improvisation is a part of life. It is also a part of creativity. It means taking risks, but it is a way of saying yes to life with all its irregularities.

Our tendency, unfortunately, is all too often to live as though we were sleepwalking. We tend to stick to the same routes, to move mindlessly over known terrain. But sometimes we find ourselves on an unfamiliar part of the journey. We may have chosen to be there, or we may have had little or no say in the matter. Either way, we are likely to feel some concern at some point—and understandably so. But the new situation can also get our attention and refocus us.

Everyone I interviewed for this book talked in one way or another about responding creatively to life. For example, Ralph, the seminar leader/business consultant whose career was brought to a halt by life-threatening illness, admitted that "it was a good/bad sort of thing, because I came to the conclusion that what I had been pursuing was an empty dream. I realized that the valuable things that in life are not the things that are achieved through the success of your career, being recognized as a leader in your field, being popular in front of audiences, or making a lot of money. All of those things become unimportant at a time when you're facing possible death. You don't know whether you're going to survive the next twenty-four hours and you're saying to yourself, `What have I really gained in all this, and what have I lost?'"

Ralph did survive the threat to his health and the death of the dream he had been chasing, only to find that he didn't know quite what to do next. For some months, he said, "I experienced some real downers in the sense of `where do I go?' Nothing was coming together." To make matters worse, Ralph's illness coincided with some very heavy financial losses, incurred through his silent partnership in a business venture separate from his own work. "Suddenly a lot of the support that I'd built into my savings and everything else had gone down. It took a lot of the polish off the personality, or the pride part of it."

After a time his response to his situation became a very methodical one. He had been sticking pretty close to home, sending out some resumes, making a few random telephone calls, often getting up after his wife went to her job. "My wife went to work, the kids were at school, and I'd be sitting around the house piddling with this and that, doing odds and ends, going around looking for work at friends' places and not achieving anything. I was waiting for the phone to ring."

But then he chose to change. "What I essentially did was to get up early the next morning, and I still remember my wife saying, `What's going on, where are you going?' It was seven o'clock in the morning and I was on my way out with my tie and jacket on, showered and shaved. I said, `I'm going to look for work.' She said, `Do you have an interview?' I said, `No, but I'll get one.'

"I started initially by going to a restaurant where there are booths, where you can sit down. I'd take my telephone directory, I'd take my notebook and my briefcase with all my stuff in there, and I would sit down and start working. I would write down names, addresses, telephone numbers, people to contact, and so on.

"I've always found it difficult to do cold calls on the telephone. So I would put ten quarters in the right pocket of my jacket in the morning, as a way of trying to force myself to make ten phone calls that day. If at the end of the day there were still some quarters left in there, they would be in that pocket the next morning with ten more. I remember that at one point I had twenty-one or twenty-two quarters in there. It was the heaviest pocket I'd ever experienced, because symbolically it meant that there were twenty-two phone calls that I was behind."

But Ralph also remembers that he found a way of rewarding himself for calls made. "If I could get into an office, borrow somebody's phone, and make a couple of contacts and get an appointment, I would then transfer, for every call made like that, a quarter out of the pocket for calls into a pocket for coffee money. That was a great experience. I very quickly learned to sponge phones wherever I could. And in less than three weeks I had three very good job offers."

As well as finding new employment, Ralph also learned some things about the job search process which are consistent with recommendations made by many career and relocation counselors. In making his calls, he said, "I learned very quickly that you don't ask for a job on the phone. Because the simple answer to that is, `No, I don't have anything.' What I did was ask to meet with people and talk with them." And his experience was that "people are willing to talk to you. They are willing to share ideas, to look at your resume, to make suggestions. I found people were very, very supportive. But don't ask for something they can't provide. In other words, don't ask for a job which they don't have. Because then they have to say no, which makes everyone uncomfortable and then the relationship isn't going to be as positive as it might be otherwise."

Ralph's story, of course, is an example of the way things are "supposed to happen"—the way we'd like for them to happen, at least as far as the job search process is concerned. But sometimes they happen differently, in ways that may seem less than successful—at least in the short run. Sometimes an individual makes all the right efforts only to find that they are not followed by the "right" results. In such cases, the important thing is to be open to different kinds of discoveries—which, in a positive sense, is a kind of surrender.

We may react negatively to the word "surrender." It may sound like nothing but defeat. But surrender, which I shall talk more about later, is primarily about trust. It includes acceptance of the cyclical, the invitation to growth implicit in all of life's necessary losses, the need for improvisation. To surrender in this context is to acknowledge the fact that we don't know how things are going to turn out, that our control over life is limited, and that overattachment to rigid expectations is counterproductive. It is to attend to the present rather than being overly concerned about the future.

One example of that kind of attitude is a man I'll call Brad. A Ph.D. in chemistry, Brad held management positions with several major corporations before being a victim of cutbacks related to the oil crisis in the 1970s. After almost two years of being unemployed, he secured a position as president of a small oil company in the southwest, only to have the position—and his job—eliminated in the mid 1980s.

"The Chairman of the Board of my company and the President of the parent corporation and I had a little chat in his office, in which we said that we would dissolve the company that I was president of. Which is an interesting way to lose your job."

By that time Brad was ready for a different kind of change. And so, following a good deal of soul-searching, he returned to his alma mater where for several years he worked as a teaching and research assistant and his wife worked as a sales clerk. Then, in his mid-50s, he began to put out feelers for a teaching position. Now, after not one but two severe career shocks, he is teaching at a small college in the southwest.

He described some of the excitement of the transition, especially the part that involved going back to school: "This was a really exciting period for me as it turned out, because I found very quickly that the old skills were there, and the same thing that had enabled me to excel in graduate school was still with me. The difference between 26 and 56 was trivial. This was a labor of love. This was something I was really enjoying. There were no more budgets and no more dealing with the creditors of a corporation—just the pursuit of an intellectual goal."

As I talked with Brad, I realized that his creative response to his employment crisis was part of a larger picture. For while chemistry is his professional love, his interests are a good deal more diverse.

"I've always been a curious person about things other than just the narrow field of chemistry. In fact, though I have always pointed toward chemistry as a field, I was perhaps equally interested in reading, literature, and my present occupation [teaching]. And early in my adult life I developed an interest in the outdoors—hiking and wilderness trips and that sort of thing. These were things that could be done with my family in many cases. I could leave the work at work. I was able to keep at these outdoor activities during my time between jobs, and I still make time for them."

Brad described himself as having a lot of self-confidence, which he feels comes from a mixture of having grown up in a supportive family and having enjoyed a number of achievements in his early life. Not everyone, of course, is so fortunate. But the important thing to note is that he has a strongly rooted view of himself which encompasses more than the world of job work.

Moreover, in the course of a transition which took place in several stages and through several job losses, Brad became more and more willing to take action while accepting that he didn't know how things would turn out. As he reviewed for me the difference between the first major job loss and the second, he remembered that at the time of his first termination he was determined to hold onto the house that he and his family owned. By the time the second crisis occurred, however, he knew that he needed to move in a new direction. He didn't know what the outcome would be, but the day he cleaned out his office he and his wife also listed their house with a real estate agent.

Finally, Brad's story is a reminder of how easy it is to lose parts of ourselves that are important—perhaps especially our creativity. For, he told me, he had come to realize that in his movement up the corporate ladder he had moved away from opportunities to be creative, which were very important to him. That realization happened to coincide with a job loss. But I suspect it might have occurred even if he had not faced an employment crisis. Changes were in order if he was to honor a vital part of himself that was being neglected.

Brad's career started out in a pretty standard way, and the "detours" came later. In the case of a man I'll call Ted, however, things were almost the reverse. For ten years prior to getting the job he now holds in the human resource field, his career path was marked by a variety of short-term jobs and by frustration at being unable to find an opening which would allow him to do human resource work—a field to which he felt a deep commitment.

While in his teens Ted had learned a craft which he pursued intermittently throughout his college years and even after he got married and had children. But, he explained to me, "I really wanted to be a counselor. I really had a drive to get into that field."

Unfortunately, however, circumstances did not permit him to get the kind of training which would have made for the usual kind of access into counseling and related work. He had been active in church and had worked with youth groups, "but making the transition from trade work as a career to the counseling field wasn't easy. And if I was working at counseling there was sometimes no income attached to it. It was often volunteer work, which was very informal and not at all highly structured in terms of being a job.

"I took a chaplaincy training program through a hospital which was helpful in terms of pastoral counseling but didn't really bridge the gap between a church background and getting work in a secular setting."

At the same time Ted was going to school, working at any jobs he could find. "I just took work that was available, regardless of what it was. Having a wife and two children meant that I was supporting them. And my wife worked when she could since we really needed two incomes.

"And one of the things I discovered was that certain work had some intrinsic value for me and other work only had monetary value for me—value that was external. I was certainly more motivated to do the work that had some intrinsic value.

"For example, I remember working at a chemical plant, filling buckets with a very potent chemical and putting them in boxes and taping up the boxes. It was a very menial job. But there were occasions when I would come home, smelling horrible from the chemicals, and would wash myself, put on a coat and tie, and go out and do a seminar on stress management.

"One time I was working the night shift and when I got off work I needed to sleep before doing a workshop that evening. And because the kids were at home I slept on a park bench, then went home, showered, and went out and did the workshop. I was motivated enough to do that because the seminar work had intrinsic value for me. I got paid for it—in fact, actually quite well—but I probably would have done it voluntarily."

Still, he was unable for years to find the kind of salaried position he needed and wanted. "I was always working, I always found something to do. I guess I didn't make the distinction between looking for work and working at some kind of job. But at one time I must have had at least five hundred rejection letters. And it really does something to you when you look at that kind of stuff and you realize it's not happening."

In the period just before a good job opening did come, he said his mood was "pure exhaustion, exhaustion of having tried so many times, and having repeatedly been forced to look at the fact that it didn't work. You tried this, you tried that, you read this, you read that. You talked to this person, you talked to that person, you tried this strategy, you tried that strategy and it still turned out negative. I think pure exhaustion for me was a sort of acceptance of `that's the way it is and you can't do anything about it.'"

But in another part of our interview, Ted acknowledged a paradox: "The job I finally got was based on a very random set of circumstances, and yet I could tell that the effort I'd put into getting into that career had some impact on the opportunity that came, and on my being able to take advantage of it."

It seems to me the significant thing here is that Ted did not see surrender as representing defeat. On the contrary, as his experience illustrates, it involves learning to avoid all-or-nothing thinking which says, at a level below consciousness, "if I cannot control everything I need not try to control anything." The object is to discern between those things which we can control and those which we cannot, and to do something about the former while letting go of the latter as graciously as possible.

Sometimes the path of creative response requires a good deal of zigzagging. Cheryl's story is an example. Cheryl's early career path, you may recall, included obsessive devotion to the profession of architecture. But in spite of her commitment and qualifications, she suffered a number of layoffs, each one more difficult than the last. And her personal life was virtually nonexistent.

Following her first layoff, she threw herself into the job search process and was successful about two weeks later in landing another job. And although she was beginning to feel that there were some inner needs that she should attend to, she continued to do "hardly anything outside of work."

But then another layoff came less than a year later. Cheryl said, "At that time I had to take unemployment. I had to do that for all of December and for most of January and I felt terrible." During that layoff period Cheryl turned 40. And, although she described her personal life as having been virtually nonexistent, a woman friend who was also an architect and who was having job problems similar to Cheryl's, "actually took me out for my birthday. And it was a very fine thing because my parents were out of the country, and I thought I didn't have anyone to be with on my birthday. I was so amazed. I didn't have any money, I was on unemployment, so I was really very, very much down."

That friend, who had recently taken a non-architectural job with the county where both she and Cheryl lived, knew of another job opening in her department. When the friend offered to help Cheryl get it, she responded positively, even though it was definitely a step "down."

"Basically, the two of us drove around in this great old yellow truck and we did drainage reviews—surface water drainage reviews for commercial sites. And we'd have these great long talks about what we were going to do with our lives."

As they talked, both women agreed that they did not want to return to architecture, primarily because of its uncertain up-and-down nature. But then Cheryl was offered what for her was an exceptional job directly related to architecture, and she took it. However, she also kept the job with the county. And later, when the man she worked for in the job related to architecture demanded that she make a choice, she chose to keep the public job.

Her reasons were very clear: "I decided not to quit the public job, first of all because of the job security and regular salary, which would let me continue therapy I had started. Also, I knew that my boss in the architectural firm was a very unhappy man who could be angry and rude and I didn't want to work around that kind of person."

Cheryl also had discovered something else which was related to the fact that her county job was far less demanding than employment in architecture had been: "I was exhausted, literally exhausted. And it was so amazing for me not to have to just come in and crank it out, to have a smile on my face, be optimistic...I could let my mind wander. I just couldn't believe that."

In short, Cheryl had gone from an obsessive commitment to "making it" in a competitive field which was unusually sensitive to boom and bust to accepting a much less prestigious job with the government. She admitted she sometimes felt embarrassed at having it, but appreciated that it was far less demanding and provided far more security. Along the way she began to deal with personal issues, including her relationship needs and her need to be more realistic about her financial situation.

Eventually, Cheryl did leave the job driving the big yellow truck. Her present one is closer to her interests in architecture and more in keeping with her abilities. But that job is with the same government department and it offers the same kind security and benefits as the old one.

Some people might be inclined to see Cheryl's career path as having gone downward. But that is to look at it through only one prism: that of the ego-driven competitive self. What Cheryl has discovered, what all of the other people I interviewed have discovered, is that there are other prisms through which to see oneself.

The point is that creativity allows for less-travelled paths and for alternate prisms. It also allows for claiming experiences as they come to us, for seeing value in the detours and in the interruptions. We sometimes speak of it as "making the best of a bad situation," or "making lemonade out of lemons."

It is what allows an individual who is stuck in traffic or a waiting room to look about and find something of interest—for example, a spectacular configuration of clouds overhead or an intriguing article in a two-year-old magazine. It's an all too rare quality, but it is possible for us to find it in ourselves.

I also heard this creative approach to life described, along with the struggle that went with arriving at it, in my interview with Peter. "I tried everything I could to find a job," he said, "but to no avail." He had been working for a small magazine, was married, and had small children.

Peter went on to talk about the fact that losing his job, and with it his role as the only salaried person in the family, was very hard. "As the male, I thought I had to be the breadwinner. I think it was a role thing, and I pretty much bought into it." He continued, "I was angry at what had happened to me and at the people who had made it happen. I was very fearful of not being able to support my family, and I was full of shame that I was not as successful and affluent as some people I knew. I thought pretty negatively of myself."

He also admitted that the experience brought home to him his limitations and vulnerability in a way he had not previously experienced. And the result, for a time, was depression. "It's the only time in my life in which I experienced that," he said. It lifted not when he got a job but "when another person, a very wise friend, made me aware that I was too fixed on the idea that I was the breadwinner. I needed to look to my wife for all that she could give in the situation and to follow her lead, which I did. At that point the real depression lifted, even though I still didn't have [a paid job] yet."

Peter went on to find other work and to resume his role as the breadwinner in his family. But he spoke almost reverently of some of the things he learned during his employment crisis. "I think I became much more vulnerable as a human being. I think it made me not take the basics of life for granted, like the chance to work. I think it made me more attentive and more vulnerable with my children and my wife.

"I think it's a very rich experience to realize that one doesn't have all the outer accoutrements to protect one's identity. Just to smile at someone or to be aware of them becomes a matter of some importance because you know that you're not falsely protected from all the human emotions. You're in the vicissitudes of life like other people are, like children are. You realize that the people to whom bad things happen are not just others." It was an awareness, he says, that "never had come home with such force before."

As he recalled his experience, however, Peter went on to say, "I think in some sort of way I accepted myself, and by that I mean I accepted that I wasn't affluent like some of the people I knew, that I was of a different temperament than affluent people usually are, and that I could see there was something about the more simple environment where I lived that was consistent with my nature.

"When I was unemployed and there were potatoes on the table, I could see that the potatoes were something I could afford and enjoy, so I didn't take the very bare essentials of survival for granted. I appreciated them. I also realized that it wasn't necessary to have a lot beyond them and that my own attitude was more important than affluence."

By alluding to attitude, Peter reminds us of a fundamental tenet of human well-being. One person who has articulated that truth well is Viktor Frankl, a psychiatrist and a survivor of Auschwitz. According to Frankl, human beings can find meaning in three principal ways.* One has to do with what a person *gives* to the world in terms of his or her creations. The second has to do with what people *take from* the world in terms of encounters and experiences. And the third involves the *stand* an individual takes in the face of predicaments and challenges which can neither be avoided nor changed.

Frankl is not arguing for passivity; in fact, he is urging quite the opposite. He is in favor of finding meaning and value by way of either of the first two options if at all possible—through action or experience. In the framework of an employment challenge, for example, people should do what they can to get another job—assuming, of course, that they want one. It is not an argument for giving up—although it does allow for accepting that we may not be able to change things in the way we would like, at least not in the short term.

But Frankl tells us that there is also a third option— namely, that meaning can be found not only by overt action but by way of our attitude, our perspective, the way in which we interpret what is happening and respond to our circumstances. That viewpoint is inherently creative. It allows us to discover meaning and purpose by exploring ways of valuing and affirming ourselves apart from the workplace.

Creativity is not magic. It does not mean bringing something out of nothing. There is a sense, however, in which it does bring things into being. Or, to put it another way, it helps us to make discoveries—whether our endeavor is writing a poem or making a life.

The creative act or response almost always involves rationality and discipline, but the urge or the impulse which engages it draws upon an energy or power that is beyond rationality and operates at a level below consciousness. The creative process, which has to do with rearranging, reconfiguring, reframing, remapping, and/or re-visioning, happens by way of a mixture of intuition, improvisation, and action.

We often feel that we must make a choice between being active or receptive. And the answer is not either/or but both/and. We need to be open to inspiration. If creativity is to become actualized, however, we have to respond to the inspiration with the energy of our best effort.

To be creative is not to be indifferent to dreams and goals. But it is to allow for the possibility that in striving to realize a dream or in moving toward a goal we may discover—or be discovered by—others that are even more meaningful for us. To be creative is to bring our energy into line with a power which is greater than ourselves—or, at the very least, which operates at a level not wholly susceptible to our control.

Let me illustrate by referring again to Norman, whom we met in the preceding chapter. Norman, you may remember, spent most of his working life in the construction business. Several years ago, however, changes in the company he worked for made it necessary for him to explore other ways of earning a living. Now he is self-employed as a photographer.

Norman is working very hard to learn to market himself and his work effectively. He is doing what he can to succeed. But his creativity is seen in his attitude as well as in his photographs. For example, he accepts that professional photography may not be the final outcome of his vocational journey. He has goals and dreams but few if any fixed expectations. Much that he said in my interview with him reflected an attitude of trust in the deeper levels of creativity. That trust, it is clear, is an important part of his way of living. But it is also clear that it was not always there.

"Whenever we went someplace I always used to carry my camera. I was afraid I was going to miss something, miss the great image. Now, if I just feel like going on a walk or whatever, doing something with my wife without the encumbrance of my camera and equipment, it seems like the universe creates an opportunity some other time to capture an image."

We hear little about that kind of approach. And yet we intuitively know that there is a "truth" and a practicality to it. To cite but a few examples: often an answer to a problem comes when we least expect it; the worst thing one can do when trying to go to sleep is to try harder; we all know couples who have given up trying to conceive a child and have adopted one instead, only to find that the woman is pregnant shortly thereafter.

This brings us up against a very challenging issue: our need for a sense of control in our lives. Which is important. It is beneficial in dealing with stress and it helps us avoid being caught in the role of victim. One of the things most frightening about a crisis of any sort is the felt loss of control. One of the advantages of employment is that it contributes to our sense of control.

The problem, of course, is that life confronts us with a hard reality, namely that we have very little control over the way in which it unfolds. We are able to influence the course of some events. Depending on our circumstances, we may be able to exercise quite a good deal of influence, and we can and should do what we can to give ourselves the best odds possible. Which includes, for example, attending creatively and conscientiously to matters affecting our health, our relationships, and our employment needs.

As we all know, however, our best-laid plans, intentions, and hopes sometimes go awry. Health fails, relationships end, jobs are lost, opportunities are missed, and promotions are given to other people. When such things happen, the path we were on can suddenly seem to be meaningless and to be leading to a dead end.

At such times it is vital that we do our best to live responsibly—which simply means taking charge of how we respond to the people, circumstances, and happenings which we encounter. It means responding as creatively and courageously as possible to the ways in which life unfolds. It is to recognize the impossibility of total control, but the reality of limited control. It is to accept that we cannot control everything but we can control some things—such as how we respond. It is to understand, moreover, that the value of a response lies as much in its quality and choices as in its outcome.

In the case of an employment crisis, one of the things you cannot ultimately control is whether or not you will be hired, promoted, or laid off. Those choices are someone else's. You may be able to influence them, but you cannot control them.

What you *can* do is engage with the challenge. Accepting that you cannot control a decision or circumstance can open the way to dealing more adequately—and realistically—with those parts of a job or job search process which are subject to your control. They include: preparation of a good quality resume, the use of networking, paying attention to job duties valued by your employer, and being well prepared for interviews. By focusing on those things, you free energy to attend to what *is* within the scope of your control. That truth, you may recall, was well illustrated by Ralph's story. He devised a workable, manageable plan—which included leaving home each morning with ten quarters in his pocket—and he stuck to it one day at a time.

We often have a greater degree of choice than we may think, and therefore some degree of control, concerning the various parts of the job-search process. And the same thing is true of other employment-related challenges—for that matter, challenges of all sorts. In some cases, granted, the choices may be limited.

But often we assume they are not there without even looking carefully.

The key thing to remember, of course, is that your control is greatest with respect to yourself. You have little if any control over what others do, how they respond, or what decisions they make. But you have a great deal of control in many areas of your own life. And the better you know yourself the better you will be able to respond creatively, to claim your priorities in ways that reflect integrity and authenticity.

This truth, it seems to me, is the foundation of effective stress management. Stress is a natural reaction to a perceived threat and, as such, is a basic resource for survival. If, for example, we see a vicious animal nearby, stress is a very healthy reaction. It activates an assortment of physiological responses—rapid heartbeat, increase in adrenaline, and others—which help us do what is necessary to protect ourselves. It is part of the so called "fight or flight" response.

Sometimes, however, we feel threatened when we don't have to—or more than we have to. And often the perceived threat is to our self-esteem. If we are criticized, slighted, or passed over for some kind of recognition, we feel threatened. Which is natural, up to a point.

But we need to remember that we have a choice in how we react. It's not that we should be passive and pretend that things don't matter when they do. But the deeper our inner sense of our true identity is, the better able we will be to respond appropriately to all kinds of stress—whether that means asserting ourselves more or choosing to interpret a slight as someone else's problem rather than our own.

Control, according to psychologist Blair Justice, is primarily a belief.* There are times when we have a sense of control even though there are no facts in support of that feeling. That feeling of control, according to physician and philosopher Larry Dossey, "seems largely to flow from an inner certainty or faith about one's place or role in life."*

Inner certainty, Dossey goes on to argue, is sometimes encouraged by religious faith—by belief in a higher power. And I would argue that it is also fostered by getting in touch with the creativity that is an integral part of who we are. Knowing ourselves in this way can give us strength and help us to stay centered in the midst of the challenges of life.

To know and exercise appropriate control is not to try to deny the stresses of life but rather to try to learn from them. It is to move from "why me?" to "what next?" It is to recognize that our dignity and our self-esteem lie not in controlling all of life through force or power—which is quite impossible—but in responding openly, creatively, and honestly to its ebb and flow. To focus on such things is not to assure any particular outcome but to assure that we have done all that we can. It is to claim the dignity and self-esteem that are present in the process.

Even if falling apart—or a sense of falling apart—is involved, we need to try to see that part of the process in perspective. We need to remember that disintegration is an integral part of the creative process, the becoming process. The disintegration is not always apparent, but it is always there. And it can allow for healing and renewal. The important thing is for us to find the help necessary for making the transition and to allow ourselves to move through the experience.

Many of the people I interviewed went through some kind of falling apart. Peter, for example, who lost his job as a journalist, had an extended period of depression, as did Frank, the former teacher who had a dream that helped him to accept himself. Both Leon and Brian felt that their respective worlds had fallen apart in connection with their job terminations in the corporate and academic worlds, respectively. Cheryl, the former architect, spoke of her anger and of doing a lot of crying with a therapist. Although Moira, the housewife who became a teacher, did not have an employment crisis, she had difficult life issues to deal with which required a good deal of time in counselling.

We are therefore brought back to the notion of surrender,

which is often associated with the process of recovering from alcoholism and other addictions. But it can also be understood in a larger context that includes creativity. In their book *Creativity in Business*, for example, authors Michael Ray and Rochelle Myers quote businessman Stephen Portis as saying that to surrender is "to let go of any emotional attachment to the final outcome."*

That understanding would seem, at first glance, to be a bit different from what is meant when an addicted person talks about surrendering. For the most obvious reference in that context has to do with accepting the reality of one's illness or condition, with ceasing to deny the problem.

And yet what is really involved is letting go of an obsession with control, which is what underlies all addiction. The obsession grows out of the perceived need to try to control the vicissitudes of life, or to have the illusion of such control. Which, in fact, almost invariably leads to *loss* of control. To surrender to one's addiction and the need to do something about it is also to let go of inappropriately trying to control outcomes.

Perhaps the most significant thing to keep in mind is that surrender, seen as a kind of dying and being reborn, can be very empowering. It is an integral part of the creative process. In most cases it happens almost unnoticed—like breathing out and breathing in, like sleeping and waking. But even when it happens more conspicuously—as, for example, in acknowledging the need for counseling or other support frameworks—it needs to be seen in light of the same overall process.

To live creatively, to respond to life creatively, is to affirm the value of surrender. This does not mean ignoring all concern for the future; to do that would be to ignore a vital part of what makes us human. Rather, it is to accept that we don't really know how things are going to turn out—and that there is value in not knowing. It is to affirm the paradox that the future is best dealt with by attending to the present.

That stance is not a passive one, and in this context it should not be thought of as being synonymous with defeat. It simply allows for improvising, for reframing—for re-visioning one's map, recharting one's course. It honors and trusts the reality and the power of our creativity. It involves taking action in the present while trusting in a process and a power greater than ourselves, however we understand or define it.

Practicing surrender, as I am using the term here, is an effective antidote for obsession with control. It allows for living as fully as possible, both in the valleys and on the mountaintops, and for finding value in *being* as well as in *doing*. It is a stance which affirms the paradoxes of life, the both/and nature of existence, and it is therefore consistent with the kind of truth found in mythology and spiritual traditions throughout the world.

At heart, it seems to me, creativity has to do with vision—not so much with what is seen but rather with a way of seeing. It is a way of approaching life, one which includes spirit, soul, ego, and self. It may involve solving problems, but it is not primarily about problem solving. It is not a means to an end, but an end in itself. It is an approach which allows for transformation and for the meandering that is often involved in making one's way toward home.

To speak of creative vision is to speak of attitude with dimensionality. Attitude has to do with angle of vision or of approach. Creative vision is angle plus depth, breadth, color, shadings, composition, and more. It is what permits the artist to show the subject as having three dimensions rather than only one or two.

To continue with the analogy of an artist and his or her subject, attitude is the position of the artist with respect to the subject; it affects how the artist "visions" the model. But that visioning, what the artist sees in the subject, also allows for paradox—for seeing beauty and value in something whose beauty and value may not be apparent to the naked eye. And more often than not it includes more than the artist knows consciously. In some sense, that is, creativity involves us at a level below consciousness.

We hear a good deal about visualization these days—a technique which is a close ally of creativity and can be quite powerful. It is used with success by many professional athletes and by some health professionals who work with people suffering from chronic illness. The idea is that we follow our inner images, and that by using them we can help to bring about the end result we want—whether it involves sinking a putt or destroying cancer cells.

I do not want to deny the usefulness of visualization—which is sometimes referred to as "imaging." Images are powerful; we do tend to follow them. They can open the way to new insights and deeper levels of experience. But they can also close the way. We may, for example, believe there is only one "right" image for ourselves. As a result, we may visualize getting another job like the one we had, when we may really want to move to something much different and more satisfying.

Thus there are times when it is best for visualization to have an open-ended quality, when it needs to allow for the unexpected, for improvisation. If we are so inclined, we may "see" a beautiful statue in what looks to anyone else like nothing but a large rock. But we need to remind ourselves that in the process of finding that statue it will almost invariably take on a life of its own.

What I am arguing is that vision and visualization are related but distinct. I don't want to overemphasize the distinction, but it seems to me the first has to do with the way of seeing while the second involves what is seen. Vision, that is, has more to do with process, visualization with the object or outcome. Creative vision, moreover, allows for visualization that incorporates paradox. The important thing to keep in mind is that visualization can be the servant of vision.

Looking back over your life, for example, you may again want to see it as a journey with many twists and turns, some of which may be more pleasant than others, but none of which needs to be cause for permanent despair. Or you may want to see it as a rich tapestry woven with bright colors, pastels, and darker shades, with some loose and frayed threads here and there but also many strong ones.

Looking ahead, you may want to visualize the talents and strengths you have which you have not yet explored. Try reinventing yourself—reframing yourself. Imagine yourself doing something different from what you previously did—working at a different type of job, at a part-time position, or working for yourself. Let yourself dream.

If appropriate, visualize the steps you can take on the road to new opportunities. Give your imagination permission to be active. (Which is what Brad, the former corporate chemist, did—even though it meant going back to school and working as a teaching assistant when he was in his 50s.) To adopt that stance—that attitude, that angle of vision—can help you to see yourself accomplishing the things that are most important to you in any aspect of life, including job work.

Trust your creative vision; let your dreams inspire you. You don't have to limit yourself to a mundane view. Remember the oft-told story of the three stonemasons. A man passed by where they were working and asked what they were doing. One said, "I'm laying stones." Another replied, "I'm putting up a wall." The third one said, "I'm building a cathedral."

As you think about making a living and a life, allow your visualization to include some open-ended dreams and imagery. See yourself building a cathedral whose design is not yet finalized. Imagine starting on a journey with no fixed destination—or at least no fixed itinerary. Allow for some side trips. Give yourself permission to be an explorer.

Doing so can serve as a reminder that you don't have to stay with ordinary strategies, paths, and plans. It can help you avoid being limited by expectations that are too rigid, avoid pinning all your hopes on a particular outcome, avoid seeing yourself as being nothing more than what you do. It can help you to make your life a work of art—which does not have to be perfect in order to be valuable.

Open-ended imagery also brings us around to the fact that

creativity suggests a paradoxical truth about selfhood. On the one hand, to be creative is to care deeply, to give of oneself without reservations. We know, for example, that people who are notably talented and creative—composers, poets, artists—are often wrapped up in their work in a way that appears to involve total identification with it. They and their work can seem to be one. And in a sense that is true.

But there is also a sense in which the artist must detach from the creative work. In the words of Stephen Nachmanovitch, author of the book *Free Play,* "for art to appear, we have to *disappear.*"* Part of that truth has to do with the fact that to enter fully into any kind of creative activity is to lose oneself—or at least to lose self-consciousness—only to discover at some point that one has gained a strengthened sense of self in the process. It is a sense of self—and of self-esteem—based not upon accomplishment but upon trust. It has to do not so much with ego as with soul. It brings us back to self-esteem derived from what is within us rather than solely from that which is external.

A related truth is that the artist—or, by implication, any person who exhibits creativity—has to get out of the way in order for his or her creation to realize its full potential. In order for the creative achievement to come to life, the one who does the creating must separate, must let go of the painting or book or composition—or the job or the work project.

That truth is also reflected in a broader sense. Our relationships with other people, for example, are strengthened not by holding on obsessively but by letting go. Parents must let go of children—and children of parents—if growth and maturity are to happen. Healthy marriages and other intimate relationships need to allow "space" for each partner. Letting go is an essential part of all growth and development.

People with healthy self-esteem are free to let go. They can assert themselves, but they do not have to be overly concerned with themselves. They are self-confident without being overly self-conscious. And commitment to that which is creative—

whether understood as a way of living or as an expression of talent, or both—helps us nourish that kind of self-esteem in that it allows us to find ourselves even while losing ourselves.

That view is quite contrary to the standard messages we get about being in control, about taking charge, and about accomplishment. But to be unable to let go, to fail to get out of the way, is to know the dark side of creativity—that part of the process which can engulf, overwhelm, literally *take over* the one who is doing the creating, and even those affected by him or her.

That side is real and destructive. And it also can be subtle, seductive, and powerful. It is present in many guises throughout our culture. It underlies the compulsion to work at a job and to define oneself in terms of greater and greater material success and power. It can result in giving of the self as a commodity—often a self which is not fully realized—and having it devoured.

True creativity, on the other hand, allows us to be in touch with our deepest, most authentic self. It opens us to a resource which can enable us to live and work with vitality. It has to do not so much with creating an original *thing* as with being an original person—with claiming and realizing our unique identity and potential.

The resource of creativity is invaluable whether the objective is finding a job, being ourselves more fully while holding down existing jobs, adjusting to retirement, or simply living with verve and enthusiasm. It can be successfully applied whether we are talking about making a life, making a living, or making a poem.

To respond creatively to the challenges and losses of life takes a blend of hope, trust, and courage. It means that we must be willing to confront the darkness as well as the light, to go beyond conventional thinking sometimes, to reframe the way in which we view our roles—and, indeed, our very selves. But the fact is that reframing happens at every stage of our growth, from infancy through childhood and adolescence and into adulthood and old age. It is an essential part of our journey.

To respond to life creatively is to open ourselves to a healing perspective. For it allows us to acknowledge pain and to grow through grief—including the grief that invariably goes with an employment transition. By doing so we can know more fully who we are and continue the process of fulfilling our potential with hope, courage, integrity, and authenticity.

To approach life creatively is to stay curious, to value all questions, including the "why?" ones. We are very good at asking those questions as children. Unfortunately, they tend to get "educated" out of us. One reason is that they often have no answer—or at least no easily discernable answer. In the face of personal calamity, for example, the most common, gut-level question is "Why me?" It is not a bad question. It is part of what makes us human. But there is really no answer to it. We are led back to psychologist Carl Jung's observation that most of the really serious problems of life are unsolvable.* We are invited, rather, to do creative soul work in response to them, which is to say to grow through them.

Part of that growth may mean reframing the question—asking, for example, "what can I learn from this experience?" The answer to even that question may not be immediately forthcoming, but the question is valuable in itself. It is an invitation to new growth, to new understanding. To approach life that way, to embrace the questions—even during a crisis—is to find a hidden source of strength. It is to respond not only to the surface events, but to the deeper meanings which may be present in them. Embracing the questions means valuing the process of living as well as the outcomes of our strivings.

As we've discussed, we encourage our creativity by accepting that we don't know how things are going to turn out, by suspending judgment about how things are unfolding and about our inner doubts, and by staying curious. And we also encourage it by practicing it.

There is really no way around that reality. We learn to walk both by believing we can walk and by walking. And the more we walk the more we believe we can walk. And so it is with our creativity. We become creative by practicing creativity—both in our attitudes and in our actions, both by viewing life through the prism of creativity and by taking time for creative self-expression.

To respond creatively is to live wide awake. It is the opposite of sleepwalking through life—which, regrettably, most of us are inclined to do. To live consciously does not promise success or ease or any of the things promised by the TV commercials. What it does offer—indeed, promises—is continuation of the spiral process which, though it invariably takes us into the depths, also helps us to move toward our full potential.

But we do not engage in this process alone—or at least we do not have to. For to live fully is to realize that we are not islands unto ourselves but are, rather, linked with others. The journey of self-discovery is about individuation—about finding and claiming our unique abilities and gifts. But we draw strength for that journey from others, and we add to our strength by sharing it with others. Which is what the next chapter is about.

Chapter Five

CONNECTING FOR STRENGTH AND PURPOSE

At the outset of this book I discussed one of the most common questions in our culture: *What do you do?* And I've talked a little about a related question, *Who are you?* Now I want to raise a few more:

What is important about what you do?
What meaning do you attach to it?
Is there purpose in your life?
Does what you do make a difference?
What matters to you deeply?

We tend to shy away from such questions. In some cases, they may make us uncomfortable. They may seem to suggest some kind of "do-good-ism" or nobleness which we don't want to ascribe to ourselves.

Or we may feel that dealing with questions having to do with meaning and purpose is simply too difficult, the answers too elusive. And so we sweep them under the rug and content ourselves with dealing with more practical matters.

If we have a job, we go back to doing it. If we don't have one, we look for one. We assume that having a job is the same as having a purpose, that in answering the question "*What do you do?*" we have said all there is to be said about purpose. Purpose in life is defined as having a job and purpose in having a job is most often seen as making money.

There is a certain truth in that stance. Job work does allow us to feel that we are accomplishing something. That is one of its prime attractions: it provides a recognizable, easily identifiable purpose and result—a paycheck. It is tangible and measurable. And focusing on job work in that way also reminds us of the importance and value of doing the things at hand.

But questions and concerns about meaning, purpose, and making a difference do surface from time to time. And while we wouldn't want to spend all of our time philosophizing about them, we do ourselves a disservice if we totally neglect them and try to deny their existence.

One thing which can prompt such questions and concerns is a job-related crisis. It may be unemployment. Or, the questions may be the result of something more subtle, such as a sense of emptiness and meaninglessness with regard to the job we are doing. In either case, we are left wondering about purpose in our lives, about whether what we've been doing has any meaning, about whether we're doing anything that makes any difference. We may even wonder if anything really matters and whether there is any way of finding meaning and purpose when one of our major support frameworks—employment—has either been pulled out from under us or has lost whatever significance it may once have had.

Those questions are important, for they have to do with our desire to make a difference. And this, in turn, has to do with the need to be needed, and, in the view of psychiatrist R.D. Laing, that need is a deep-seated part of our human makeup.* Thus it affects our self-esteem, our sense of identity. If we are to know healthy self-esteem, we need to live out values which are important to us and we need to do so in a way which permits us to feel that we are accomplishing something or making some sort of difference.

I said earlier that job work allowed us to feel that we are accomplishing something. And in some cases the accomplishment involved has a purpose which may not only be practical but noble. I am thinking, for example, of parents for whom job work is important in that it provides the most basic of human needs for themselves and those they love and are responsible for—food and shelter and clothing. In many such cases, there is virtually no choice but to pursue, with singlemindedness and to the exclusion of everything else, whatever paid work that is available.

In that context, it seems to me, we see the dignity of job work exhibited more clearly than usual. It comes not so much from the particulars of the job, but from the motivation behind doing it. For its purpose is survival—or something very close to it. It has about it concern for the continuation and well-being of one's family.

But it would be a mistake to think that job work only has this kind of purpose for those living at the subsistence level. Many people work and continue to want to work to make reasonable, non-extravagant improvements in their lives and to provide their children with opportunities that they did not have. In such cases, integrity is clearly the operative factor. Keeping up with one's neighbors is not at issue. Inappropriate ego needs are not involved.

In many employment situations, the meaning we get from what we contribute to our jobs is intertwined with what we take from them. We may feel that we are making a difference, that our lives have some significance, because of both the ability and time we bring to our job work and the fact that we take from it, at the very least, monetary reward. The fact that we value this monetary reward in terms of how it satisfies not only our wants and needs but those of others helps to explain why we become attached to our job work.

We see this truth even if the "bottom line" kind of making a difference has been wearing thin. We may, for example, have been feeling taken for granted. As we get caught up in consumerism, we may feel that we are nothing but an economic entity, even in the home. It may seem that we are spending more time trying to make more money to buy more things which mean less. We may find it easy to identify with the weariness suggested by the bumper sticker which reads, "I owe, I owe, so off to work I go."

Even in such a situation, however, we will often cling to job work. And the reason has to be understood not only in terms of the sense of identity we get from the job, but also because it allows us to feel that we make a difference. That need is a very basic one.

You may remember the earlier analysis I did of the components of job work. I suggested that the elements involved in its value to us are related to pleasure and satisfaction in the work itself and to financial reward. And the importance of the latter may well be to provide for those we care about. The real purpose involved goes beyond monetary reward. We want to have a paycheck, but we really want to do some good, to make a difference. Job loss is therefore even more than a loss of money and a felt loss of identity. It involves a loss of meaning and purpose.

Unfortunately, of course, we can confuse making a difference with purpose defined in a very narrow way. For example, a person may have as his or her purpose a material goal of some sort, such as becoming a millionaire by a particular age.

Purpose in that context tends to be concerned with security, with comfort, with excessive pride, with the need to prove something; it is the kind of purpose that is concerned with winning at the expense of others, with measuring success by the number of "toys" that one has. It is the kind of purpose that consistently refuses the call to new life, the kind alluded to by the mythologist Joseph Campbell when he spoke of those who become very successful outwardly only to find that their world has become a "wasteland of dry stones."*

But any time purpose spills over into wanting to make a genuine difference, we are into the realm of *connectedness.* It makes no sense to talk about making a difference in isolation. The very phrase, *making a difference,* implies a framework that goes beyond the individual.

Wanting to make a difference suggests an awareness that we are in some sense part of a whole not only with respect to other human beings but with all of life—and that neither our strength nor our purpose can be fully realized except in that context.

This is not to deny the importance of individual values. It is simply to say that seeing ourselves as nothing but islands unto ourselves is a limited and limiting view. Wanting to make a difference reminds us of that truth. It invariably has a social dimension; it invariably involves some sense of connectedness. We do not define ourselves adequately through relationships alone, but neither can we define ourselves adequately apart from our relatedness.

Thus, as we struggle to move beyond what I am terming the self-as-job syndrome, we need to remind ourselves of that truth. For it is a key element in helping us to find purpose beyond paychecks.

To explore the importance of connectedness is to stress at least two things. One has to do with finding strength. That happens, at least in part, through connectedness—or, more accurately, through community. And the second is that seeing ourselves as part of a larger whole can remind us that there is an arena much bigger than the workplace in which to offer our gifts and our strengths. Making a difference doesn't have to be limited to the world of paychecks and job work. There are needs all around us awaiting our response.

Unfortunately, ours is a culture which does not place much of a premium on connectedness and community. Its dominant values are individualism and competition. And so for some people, perhaps men in particular, admitting to any needs that are not financial is difficult. Such an admission seems to fly in the face of the perceived need many men have to appear strong, self-confident, and independent.

Yet acknowledging and meeting our need for others is recognized by virtually all health care professionals as crucial to human well-being—especially during times of crisis. Doing so can be of immense value as we wrestle with the "valley" feelings I identified in Chapter Two: grief, shame, fear, loneliness, anger, regret, a sense of failure, betrayal and disillusionment.

One person who emphasizes that truth is a psychologist by the name of Julius Segal, who has worked extensively with former prisoners of war, hostages, and other survivors of extraordinary stress. In his book, *Winning Life's Toughest Battles,* Segal speaks unequivocally of supportive communication with others as being a healing and strengthening "lifeline for survival"* which can be beneficial in dealing with stress and with many physical ailments.

And Robert Veninga, a professor in the School of Public Health at the University of Minnesota, echoes the same conviction. "If you want to survive a tragedy," he says simply, "you need a friend."* You need at least one individual—and perhaps more than one—whose knowledge of you goes beneath and behind the roles you play and the masks you wear and whose acceptance you can count on.

That kind of communication, that kind of connectedness, is also of importance to developing self-esteem and a sense of identity that is more than our socioeconomic persona. For as we seek to nourish identity from within we have to find people and places in which we can safely let that identity show. We need opportunities for connectedness at a level deeper than ego.

Those opportunities are seldom to be found in most work settings. While it is true that employment often provides a social component, the nature of most of the business world is such that friendship more often happens in spite of it than because of it. That fact is probably true even at the best of economic times. And when the economic situation is such that the people who have jobs are very fearful of losing them, the atmosphere in the workplace is even less conducive to forming deep friendships.

Human interaction in the workplace tends to be based on our external identity—on the the positions we occupy and the jobs we do. And the operative framework, whether overt or not, is competition. Which is by no means all bad, but neither does it encourage the kind of interaction which can be healing and empowering.

The workplace lends itself to labels—to the assumption that people can be known by the tags or badges they wear. In the workplace we need quick and easy ways of identification, and in that kind of setting (the character of which often spills over into the broader social environment), there is neither the time nor the perceived need to know people more completely, to know their stories.

Granted, there are exceptions. People who work together over long periods of time sometimes do get to know each other reasonably well. But the nature of most job work settings does not really encourage relatedness having much depth. What is important in job work settings is getting the job done, and thus there is not a lot of time for getting to know each other in terms of where we have come from and what our personal concerns, values, and priorities are.

One of the themes that surfaced a number of times in my interviews with men who had spent much of their professional lives in large corporations was the absence of genuine caring in many such workplaces. Brian, the former university administrator, spoke of "mainlining a kind of poison when I went off to work in a big organization." And, he continued, "I decided that poison isn't good for me, and so I'm not going back to that kind of atmosphere."

Brad, the former corporate chemist, spoke of big organizations as having "a lousy atmosphere, in which you can make your way if you're confident but only if you have your guard up all the time, particularly if you're working anywhere near the upper levels."

And Sam, the former executive who concluded he didn't want the top position he'd spent most of his life striving for, expressed the view that in order to be successful in the corporate world, you must have power. "And in order to have power, trust goes out the window."

In our interview Sam also talked about the fact that the corporate environment, as he experienced it, was based on competition, even when that fact was camouflaged. "We talk about men having to be team players," he said. "Corporations talk about team players. But it's strange because while you're supposed to be a team player, you're supposed to win, and the two don't go together. The *team* can win, or should win, but we don't look at things that way. You feel *you* have to win, which means you have to screw the rest of the team, but you're still supposed to be a team player."

And so it is that we need communities, families, support groups, and friends with whom we can share our stories and come to discover who we are more fully. Those resources are worth seeking out—even if it takes some effort. We not only need to know our stories, we need to be able to share them safely. And we need to be able to listen to the stories of others.

For many people, the kind of supportive framework which is so important to human well-being will be found in traditional settings: within intimate relationships, in family settings, in churches, synagogues, and other religious communities. All of those are important and potentially valuable. But there is at least one caveat.

Although some family units will be strengthened by stress and crisis, not *all* will be, and the same is true of any other close-knit group. In some cases, the effect will be quite the opposite. We need to understand, therefore, that in some situations those closest to us may be unable to be as supportive and accepting as they might like to be.

We should also remember that people we reach out to need to be those we can trust—and who are willing and able to offer acceptance and encouragement. They should be people we have something in common with and who genuinely like us. They should exhibit some measure of inner strength themselves, and know the importance of respecting confidences. In some cases, seeking out a professional counselor may be in order. In other situations, a support group may be helpful.

Making a difference is part of the journey of self-discovery. The paradox of learning about ourselves, however, is that while it has a connectedness dimension that is very important it is something we must do for ourselves. No one else can do it for us—just as no one else can make a difference for us. And so, in being open to new and deeper types of relationships, the idea is not to seek our primary affirmation from others—or from any source outside ourselves. To do so leads to unhealthy dependency.

The legitimate search for connectedness, it seems to me, is for companionship on a journey. That companionship, if it is to be most helpful, needs to be based on the understanding that soul work—which is what the journey is all about—benefits from relatedness and community but also requires solitude.

The journey of self-discovery takes one along a solitary path with a social dimension. It is another one of those truths which is not either/or but both/and. In colloquial terms, "You alone can be well, but you can't be well alone."

Increased recognition of the importance of personal relationships—and of having failed to recognize their importance earlier—was a motif running through the stories of many of the people I interviewed. Brian, for example, thought back with more than a little sadness to the nature of his family relationships during the height of his career. "I think my daughter would say that at certain points in her life I was invisible. I heard my sons complain too that I was not available to them. I've always had a kind of commitment to some voluntary activity outside the university, and that was always taking my time.

"We took summer holidays together, but not very long ones. I never took a month off or that sort of thing, so emotionally I don't think there's any doubt that my job dominated my life to a very large extent. When other members of my family wanted to get my attention they would have to have some sort of crisis before I'd even be aware of what was going on."

Today, Brian's roles as husband and father are more prominent in his life. He spoke fondly and appreciatively of all of the members of his family, and it is apparent that communication with them has taken on a new priority in recent years. "I like my role as the father of my three kids, none of whom I live with, but I see a lot of them. I work with one of them, and I really like that. I like being a husband. I know better than ever that my wife is just a very interesting person to live with." And, he continued, "One of my jobs today is to create or recreate a personality which is as full of joy as possible and to get a kick out of the people around me."

Those people include members of several therapy groups and support groups that Brian has been part of over the past few years. They also reflect a change in his social priorities. "I've found that my tastes have changed, and that some people have just dropped out of my life and have been replaced by others who are in some sort of development process and are articulate about it."

A similar sort of pattern is evident in Cheryl's story. As you may remember, the turning point in Cheryl's career life came as a result of the friendship she developed with another female architect. That friendship was instrumental in her taking a non-architectural job with a government department. And her subsequent career moves have been consistent with the increasingly clear insights she has developed concerning her needs and priorities.

That clarity has come in part from counseling—which has included work on issues ranging from personal boundaries to finances. And it has gone hand in hand with developing a set of friendships, which now constitutes a major priority in her life. She described a particular group of them as "my extended family, six or eight or ten of them that are there for me and I'm there for them. And they're the same people who have also had some major changes in their lifestyles and have gone through some counseling. So we all understand the importance of friends."

She continued, "For example, one of my two best friends is a woman who heads up a group that delivers babies and the other one is her partner, who is a physician. They've asked me to be present at the birth of their first child, knowing that I won't be having a child. That's the kind of affirmation I find in that group."

And Ted, the person who struggled so hard to get a job in the field of human resource work, reflected on his ten-year transition period and told me he realized, "that in those times the basic elements of life take on a heck of a lot more meaning than they do when things are going well. The relationships that you have become vital to what's meaningful to you because the work's not there."

And he also recalled, "I tended to go for walks—to the zoo, to the beach. Because I had time I sometimes got into some pretty deep conversations with people in those settings. And under those circumstances, that connectedness, however brief it was, really became a form of spirituality for me."

The tendency of many of us, perhaps men especially, is to try to "go it alone" when faced with a crisis. It is part of our North American heritage. And, as I have noted, aloneness is a dimension of our journey. In general, however, it seems to me we are coming to understand and accept the importance of community and connectedness. We are becoming more aware of the need to communicate in a way that goes beyond our standard social interaction. I believe that fact helps to account for the willingness of more and more people to seek out the help of support groups and counselors. Of course, it may be true that there are more problems today, more stresses. But it may also be that we simply feel the need to have someone really listen to us.

For many people I talked with, some form of counseling or psychotherapy has been a significant part of their ongoing growth and learning. These are resources that should be sought out if problems persist and become chronic. No book is a substitute for needed professional care.

And it is also important to remember that one does not have to be suffering from a chronic condition to benefit from counseling or therapy. Simply a desire to understand oneself better is justification enough. Furthermore, the world of psychotherapy has changed greatly in recent years, and more options are available now than ever before.

If you decide to seek professional assistance in dealing with problems and pursuing personal growth, try to take a bit of time to acquaint yourself with the options. In some cases, you may be able to obtain information by word of mouth. You can also learn a good deal from reading. Finally, do not hesitate to be selective in the therapist you choose. You have every right to deal with a person you can trust—and to avoid those you don't. The point to remember is that reaching out for help isn't a sign of weakness. On the contrary, it should be seen as evidence of strength and maturity. It should be understood in the context of our connectedness with others and with all of life.

We don't exist only for ourselves. We don't make a difference in isolation. Finding purpose in living *always* takes us beyond ourselves and our individual concerns, however valid they may be. That truth is a time-honored one, affirmed in various ways by all of the world's spiritual traditions over the centuries. We gather strength for the journey from each other, and we offer strength for the journey to each other.

As we move toward a new century and a new millennium it seems especially appropriate that we remember that truth as a way of discovering ourselves. Community is the context in which we find strength, and it is also the context in which we find purpose beyond paychecks. It is the framework in which the both/and nature of creative vision gets worked out. In the framework of genuine community, we discover that our limitations can be transformed into gifts of real value.

Let me illustrate what I am talking about by using mutual help groups as an example. Sometimes called self-help groups, they embody in a down-to-earth way the time-honored spiritual principle that the journey of self-fulfillment includes caring for others.

But caregiving does not always mean a strong person caring

for a weak one. It can also consist of people caring for each other out of their mutual limitations, and finding strength in the process. In a meeting of Alcoholics Anonymous, for example, a person is valuable precisely because he or she is an alcoholic. The sharing one does in that kind of setting is as much for the sake of the person doing the sharing as for the one who is the recipient. In that kind of situation (as is true also of a love relationship), giving and receiving become one. We give by receiving and we receive by giving.

That kind of dynamic is different from what most of us are used to. We tend to think in terms of contrasts: physician and patient, teacher and student, qualified person and unqualified, professional and non-professional, strong and weak. Those on one side of the equation do the "offering;" those on the other do the "receiving."

Certainly that kind of tiered structure is almost always the operative one in job work settings. In their occupations, people are able to "make a difference" because of their qualifications. Which is as it should be. One does not want to put faith in an unqualified engineer, an unqualified surgeon, electrician, or airline pilot.

The point I want to make, however, is that there are different *kinds* of qualifications and that in some cases, a kind of paradox is involved. In the arena of war, for example, woundedness is not an asset. (And the same thing is true of most workplaces.) But in the context of life itself, those who have been wounded may have something uniquely valuable to offer.

I am not trying to glorify or romanticize woundedness. But as we think about matters of meaning and purpose, of self-esteem and identity, of job work and work having to do with selfhood behind and beneath one's persona, it seems to me we need to remind ourselves of ways of approaching life that have to do with more than traditional bottom lines. The latter are important. They cannot and should not be ignored. But neither should they be the only instrument of measurement.

One example of woundedness and of living with purpose—very familiar to almost all Canadians, but less so to others—is that of Terry Fox, a young man who had terminal cancer. Part of Terry Fox's response to that very painful reality, discovered shortly after his eighteenth birthday, was to set out in 1981 on a run across Canada to raise money for cancer research.

To those who knew about it, the run initially seemed to be a foolhardy project. But Terry Fox was a determined young man and so he did set out on his run. And, as news of his courage spread across Canada, so did support—for cancer research and for Terry Fox. Death prevented him from completing his project; he had to abandon it just outside Thunder Bay, Ontario, where today there is a marker commemorating his courage and spirit.

But an important aspect of Terry Fox's story is the reminder it gives to us that purpose does not depend on the completion of a goal to be real and important. I believe it is safe to say that Terry Fox did what he did one day, one step at a time, hoping to complete his project, but at the same time affirming by his action the significance of the process. He saw a need and he saw a way of responding to that need. It was, to my way of thinking, another example of "calling" in the comprehensive sense that I have discussed elsewhere.

One does not have to do anything as dramatic as Terry Fox did in order to live with purpose. What is significant is that he chose to respond to life with courage and creativity—which is what purpose is all about. And that is the same kind of option open to anyone—with or without a job, with or without the prompting of a major life crisis.

Living with purpose happens by attending to the present. It happens *now.* And it does not happen without a blend of courage and trust. We find those strengths, in turn, not by denying our own experience but by affirming it. Which allows us to give of ourselves, in a sense to "lose" ourselves, only to find a new and more authentic sense of self.

The point is, we have a choice. By becoming interactive, by

engaging with circumstances, by dialoguing with life, we can quite literally help to create—or co-create—our lives and the world around us. We do not have to stay stuck in the stance of the victim.

You may be surprised to learn that this does not necessarily mean that we have to *do* a lot, or that we must live out purpose through activism. Living with integrity can make a difference in the fabric of society even if we choose not to *do* anything overt. In fact, it is possible to concentrate so much on our *doing* that we fail to allow time to nourish the energizing power of our *being*.

Sometimes a transition period reminds us of that reality and invites us to correct it. For example, Judith, who left the corporate track and now is co-owner of a motorcycle shop, described herself as being much more centered as a result of forcing herself to do "nothing" for an extended period of time. It was during one of his in-between times that Brad, the corporate chemist turned university professor, took up hiking and renewed his love of the wilderness. And Peter, remembering the loss of his job as a journalist, talked of how his inner life was strengthened by paying more attention to things he had taken for granted—his wife and children, potatoes on the table, his own vulnerability.

Yet another example of the interconnection between one's inner journey and the larger environment is seen in the story of Richard, who at the time I interviewed him had been unemployed for more than two years.

Richard received a doctorate in adult education from a major university in 1991. After a bit of traveling, he and his wife chose a city in which they wanted to live and settled there. He began exploring employment opportunities in the training and human resource field.

He has made use of the strategies contained in a number of well-respected books having to do with the job search field. He has explored self-employment options as well as possible opportunities in both academic and corporate settings. His wife has been able to find short-term employment, but they are at the point of wanting to start a family and are reluctant to do so until Richard is employed.

That kind of story, of course, is not uncommon these days. What is a bit uncommon, however, is the way in which Richard sees the situation. Admitting that having his own "agenda" is not new to him, Richard explained that in graduate school he wanted to study the relationship between creativity and how people learn, and "I was going to do that regardless of whether there was a lot of support for it." He did, in fact, do his research in that area, and his interest in it has continued and expanded and he is convinced that it has practical applicability in a variety of settings.

At the risk of not doing justice to Richard's ideas, they basically have to do with problem-solving, with how to facilitate creative discoveries, and with what can be learned from those things about how people learn. He believes he will eventually find an employment setting in which they can be explored and developed further and put to practical use for the benefit of individuals, groups, and, indeed, society as whole.

But for now, Richard is using his experience as a kind of research opportunity related to his ideas. He is seeing what he can learn about them from observing his own process of problem-solving. Which does not change the fact that he gets discouraged. But he perseveres, sending out resumes, following up leads, doing all of the things that unemployed people do.

Part of what keeps him going is what he describes as "a kind of creeping expectation, because I send out all these resumes and by the time they filter back that no, they're not interested, I've already sent out a new batch. So it's just sort of a continuous process and surely the next batch will bring something."

And his interest in and commitment to something greater than himself is also significant. "I think the real kernel [of strength and hope] that I keep drawing on is that I continue to explore some issues and discover processes and creativity and what's involved in them, and I apply those things to what they could mean for promoting personal development, kind of using myself as a guinea pig for my own ideas. I guess there's this feeling that there's something valuable there and that even if no one else sees it, I think it's there, so if it's going to be developed, I'm the one who has to develop it."

Richard also talked further about his sense of purpose, his wanting to find new ways to help people develop their creative potential. "For example, if people are doing artwork, then they're doing something more for themselves, and maybe they're more alive when they have more of a sense of being or purpose. What would it mean to have a community of learners like that, and how might they be catalysts for each others' creativity and come up with innovative solutions for dealing with problems? I see this approach as part of a larger process which would hopefully make the world a better place to live. I'm onto something I think will be useful, so yes, I have a sense of purpose that this is valuable, that it has important ramifications, and that I should keep working at it."

Richard also told me that he had recently come across an encyclopedia which lists a lot of the world's problems and includes chapters on possible solutions to them. And, he suggests, it might not be a bad idea for people to approach their life's work by identifying the problems that claim their attention and trying to respond to them.

"If you could find the particular problems that interest you and think about how you could contribute toward solving them, then work becomes a way of meeting those problems. And if you can't find a job, that's not your main goal anyway. Your main goal would be to try to work with those problems, so that if you can't find a job that would ideally support you to solve some problems, you work at something else. You still work on those problems in your time spent away from supporting yourself. But you've got a larger focus in mind that's giving you direction. In that sense, your identity isn't tied up with your paid work. You do whatever it takes in order to support your larger vision. It's the larger vision that's important, not the means that you're using the bring in the money to support yourself at the same time."

Idealistic? Yes. Risky? No doubt. Refreshing? Definitely. And one other comment Richard made is reminiscent of a viewpoint about failure which I mentioned earlier: "I think it's good to have high ideals, and if they don't work out that's OK. Maybe those failures will help you deal with others over the long run. There's an old saying about creativity, that if you're not failing 50% of the time you're not trying hard enough."

Not everyone I talked with was as articulate as Richard about purpose, about wanting to make a difference. One kind of response came from a man I'll call Keith, who, after many years of being unemployed, is now a civil servant. When I asked him if he had a purpose, Keith rather brusquely said, "No." But then, as I continued the interview, he went on to express satisfaction at getting calls from people who tell him he's the only person in his line of work that they can talk to and understand.

In his case, a sense of purpose seems to go hand in hand with his employment. But what he is really talking about has to do not so much with doing a particular kind of job as with being a particular kind of person.

Whether or not a well-articulated sense of purpose and meaning was present, one thread that ran through the stories told by the people I interviewed was a willingness to respond—a willingness to engage, creatively and courageously, with life as it unfolded for them. Crises, including those having to do with employment, became for them a call to search within themselves for greater integrity and authenticity, for a deeper sense of who they are and who they could become.

Seldom if ever was that call understood solely in terms of their own benefit. Without even realizing it, most of them were committed to sharing whatever strength they might have discovered on their journey with others. Their stories remind us that the truly heroic quest is about not only finding ourselves but giving of ourselves.

Ralph, for example, talked about taking time to do church work. Judith is making a living as co-owner of a motorcycle shop, in part because it gives her maximum freedom to be active in social causes important to her. Cheryl, the former architect, speaks of her friends as extended family and of *being there for them* as they are for her. Moira, in becoming a counselor, sought to share with others the healing she had discovered in therapy.

In every case, choices were involved. And the choices did not always lead down clearly defined paths. In fact, in most cases, the opposite was closer to the truth. Take, for example, the experience of Eric and Lisa—whose story is another one that is still in the stage of conspicuous unfolding. It reminds us that following less worn paths, while often satisfying and good for the soul, is not always easy.

Eric is a university professor who, after a year's sabbatical, chose to return to his academic post but on a part-time basis. Lisa, his wife, is an artist and musician who gives private lessons and works part-time as a salesperson. But they are also working on other issues—having to do with their relationship with each other, with employment, and with the wider community.

For Eric, university teaching was the natural course of development for him. And for Lisa, too, there was a clear sense of direction in terms of her music. "I never thought of a career," she said. "Basically, what I do is paint and play the flute. Since I was nine years old, those things have been my passions. I always knew what I wanted to do. It's sort of the way I look at everything. Most of our years together I've had maybe one show a year, sometimes more, and I pretty well made my own work. I can think of doing lots of other things, but I can't think of being happier inside." She admitted, however, that it's very lonely work "and so I took an outside job so that I would realize there are other people in the world."

Over the better part of the past decade, both Eric and Lisa have been looking for outlets which would allow them to share their interests and talents in other ways. "About ten years ago," Eric said, "when our relationship hit a crisis, we really began talking about 'Well, what are we here for, not just as individuals, but as a couple? What's the point of it all?'

"So one of the physical things we did to rearrange our lives in answer to that question was to take over the second floor of our house—which had been rented since we acquired it. We no longer needed the rent from the second floor to help meet the mortgage payments, and so we turned it into a small performance space where we could do musical presentations, workshops, conversation groups, a variety of things.

"Over the past few years we've put on programs up there. But those programs have been in fits and starts around the demands of my job and other demands. We would work in a frenzy for a week or month to present something, and thirty or forty people might come for a couple of nights, and then it was over.

"Somehow there was no continuity to it. When the time was available we found that there were a lot of things that we enjoyed together and that we did well together, but we couldn't find a focus, something that would express us and carry us through the week."

For Lisa, part of the problem is that life continues to be too centered around Eric's job work. But she also added, speaking of their search for a new and sustainable direction, "I think we've been trying too hard. For example, we put so much emphasis on having an image of what we want. But part of the problem is that when you start having an image, you're measuring everything against that.

"I think what we have to do now is put all of the ideas and images and projections aside and just try to manage together, and do the things that we like to do and see what comes out of that instead of trying to plan the things that we both decide we should be doing."

Eric, who has considered giving up his university position

but is reluctant to do so because of the financial security involved, pointed out that "in many cultures, there's no word for work. You simply do what you do in the course of the day. It fits into how you relate to each other and to the land. And to me that would be a much more natural sort of thing."

Both Eric and Lisa admitted that making out of the ordinary choices is difficult. "But I think the support comes out of what you do," Eric said, "because when we do something that we really enjoy, people come and enjoy it, and we share a lot."

Lisa also talked a bit about her work as a salesperson in a mineral store and about some of the standard views of employment. "I have a friend who is a professional and is out of work. His wife has a store and for him it's a disgrace to work in her store."

This was in contrast to her own experience: "I've found that taking this job working in a store has taught me so much about humility and how much one learns when you're in a position that nobody really cares about. It somehow equalizes you to a point where you can be available to every kind of person. In a way, what you get paid to do, what you do to pay the rent and put food on the table, could be almost anything. You don't have to invest all your time and identity in your employment."

Finally, Lisa discussed the energizing power of creativity, surrender, and losing self and finding self. "When I'm drawing," she said, "there's a kind of basic energy that I feel—that I've felt doing those kinds of things since I was a child. They produce a kind of vitality. And to me that kind of flame or energy has to do with being spiritual. At those times I feel I don't have an identity. I think that all of this concern about having a specific outer identity is what kills what's really spiritual about us."

There is no doubt that there is a tenuousness about the choices Lisa and Eric are making—and about their way of life as a whole. They acknowledged that they have given less attention to financial security than they might have. And, although they have successfully offered a number of seminars out of their home, they admitted that they have not been able to market what they have to offer as effectively as they would like.

But there have also been positive developments. One has been a clearer understanding of the nature of work—and of the interconnection between work and play. Eric talked about learning to see "my [job] work as play. I'm very much part of a culture that sees work as something that you have to do, and the more you do it but don't like it the more admirable you are.

"But the last few years I really feel like I'm beginning to get past that and realize that I can work bloody hard and enjoy it, and that it's okay to enjoy it, and it's okay to be working hard in the garden. And I understand that work in the garden is real work, and I don't feel as if I'm not really working when I'm in the garden."

In a slightly different way, Lisa returned to an earlier theme to echo his sentiments. "I think that we are more than our job and more than what we even imagine we are. When I play music or make up music or draw, I'm having the time of my life. I don't feel like it's work at all. I'm not so arrogant as to think that I can change the world, but I feel like what I can do as a person is hope that I will connect [what I have to offer] with other people."

And Eric added: "People ask what you do, not where you come from. We've been so busy making money to buy the things that we should be *doing* for other people. If you bake a pie and sell it, that's part of the economy. But if you bake it for yourself or your family or friends, it's not. It's an expression of love. The same would be true if you're digging a garden or cutting hair—or whatever. There is an economy which doesn't have to do with money, but which somehow may express better what people's work should be."

In response to my question about having a purpose, Eric answered this way: "I guess if I have a purpose it's to be a human being who can be with others without judgment and with forgiveness. That's the only way to be alive, really alive. I guess that's why Lisa and I are partners, because it's challenging and immediate and every day with one other person, but it's something that you're sort of practicing for everyone else. I try to keep reminding myself of that as I go about all the things I do—the teaching and writing that I do, the music that I also enjoy playing, going and meeting someone in the store and the way I can relate to that person—that's a really important purpose for me."

One of the things I have been stressing in this chapter is that the drive to find meaning, purpose and to make a difference is part of our human nature and thus an element in our self-esteem. It at once contributes to our sense of individuality and to our sense of being connected to others and to the environment in which we live. And we find purpose and meaning and are enabled to make a difference by affirming our experience as a whole. To illustrate that truth, let me turn, once again, to Sam's story.

Sam, as you may recall, is the former corporate executive who now spends part of his time teaching people how to do their own electrical work. He is also the one who talked about the need to be needed and how he was finding ways of meeting that need outside of the job work setting. And there is yet more to his story. For, in addition to health problems of his own, Sam has had to deal with the death of a son from AIDS.

He talked of that latter experience with candor—of caring for his son at home, of being able to share deeply with him in the last months of his life, and of the further "work" to which the experience has led him.

"Because we cared for him at home until he died, and we nursed him here, I was able to say `Goodbye.' I was able to share a lot of things, we were able to come a lot closer in a lot of ways than we'd ever been. All the shit was out of the road, we had time to share and to do silly things, say goodbye."

Part of Sam's life now consists of working as a volunteer for an organization which provides home care for people dying of AIDS. He speaks of this work as "a very emotional thing, because the person you're caring for becomes part of your extended family. And they're dying, and you can't do anything about it. But it's also beautiful, because you've touched another life. You've helped a person live their life to their fullest. They're dying, but they're living. The two seem to be totally opposite, but they're not.

"Families have a difficult time dealing with death in the family to start with," Sam continued, "but fathers have a greater difficulty if at the same time they find out that their son is homosexual and has AIDS. Our society teaches that that's some kind of a stigma and a horrible thing. So I've dealt with a lot of fathers who have real serious emotional problems dealing with that. A son that they really loved yesterday they feel they have to hate today.

"If I'm able to help one father re-examine things so that he's able to deal with his feelings about his son, then I feel that's something well worthwhile to me. I recall one man I dealt with who was terrified to hug his son, and lo and behold he got ill and was diagnosed as having a brain tumor, and he had never hugged his son. Fortunately, we had talked quite a bit and he allowed himself to see that he was thinking `business as usual,' `sons don't cry,' `fathers don't cry for sure.'

"But he learned to hug his son, and they got really close. He died two weeks after the first time he hugged his son. He died, but they had shared the full two weeks that they never would have shared if he had not been able to deal with himself and his feelings. I hope I was able to open some of those doors for him, or help him open them. I'm not saying I did such great things. But I guess I listened, which was important to me."

Sam's story, it should be noted, is a prime example of a point I have emphasized a number of times—namely that one can be productive and have a purpose apart from job work. For Sam, that truth was realized through working with those afflicted with and affected by AIDS. But the specifics are not what is important. What is important is the willingness to live with purpose and to realize the range of opportunities present for doing so.

And let me specifically emphasize that stories such as Sam's in no way negate the fact that the option of living with purpose can be exercised in highly traditional ways. Keeping a roof over one's head, being able to feed and clothe the people we love—those are worthy purposes and ones that often require enormous commitment and imagination to realize. The key factor in living with purpose and making a difference is a perspective which includes other people as well as oneself. But many people, unfortunately, do their job work day in and day out without any sense of purpose or meaning—without any sense of their own value beyond a paycheck. They have the means to live but no clearly defined meaning or purpose. These are people who may, in fact, dislike their job intensely. But when it is gone, they often feel that they have nothing left. And they assume that the only way to find any meaning is to return to a type of effort that had become almost meaningless before they lost it.

Yet a significant part of finding ourselves consists of finding purpose, meaning, and a way of making a difference. And in many cases—more than we think—we can choose to live with purpose that goes beyond our paycheck.

We can do our best to respond creatively and responsibly to the needs of the people and communities we care about and to the needs of the planet we inhabit. We can choose to affirm and nourish our connectedness with others. We can experiment with "self-forgetfulness"—with putting aside our concerns for a time in order to be able to respond to the needs of others.

We can become more imaginative. We can discover not only that making a life is about more than making a living, but that attention to the former puts the latter in a new perspective. We can embrace the questions, open ourselves to discovering a "why" for living. In doing so, we may find that we open ourselves to new "how" options as well.

We should remember that our desire for purpose and meaning, for wanting to make a difference grows out of the question, "Who am I?" Each of us, if he or she is to be fully human, must try to answer that question. But we cannot really answer it by ourselves. For the answer unfolds, at least in part, in the process of discovering that we give by receiving and receive by giving, that we gain strength from others and offer strength to others. It is not that we live for ourselves *or* for others. The truth is that they are interrelated. Finding ourselves goes hand in hand with finding the willingness and courage to let go of our concerns at times and respond to those of others.

This does not mean that we should neglect our own needs. On the contrary, it is to recognize the importance of affirming and caring for all parts of ourselves, for our whole person—the value of which cannot be measured in monetary terms. In the next chapter we will discuss that kind of care in greater depth.

Chapter Six

CARING FOR THE WHOLE PERSON

Most of us know about taking care of a part of ourselves—the economic, status-concerned part. That is not surprising. We are given lots of encouragement and lots of advice on how to keep that part alive and well, on how to meet our material needs. Essentially, that advice boils down to giving ourselves unreservedly to job work—or to a role supportive of someone else's job work—so we can pick and choose from a tantalizing array of consumer goodies. The emphasis is on doing more and having more.

What we sometimes forget, however, is that we have other needs, and that our needs are not limited to the material realm.There are various ways of grouping them, but, for our purposes here, let's simply call them physical, mental, social, psychological, and spiritual.

Obviously, those needs blend, merge, and overlap with each other. Our need for intimacy, for example, has both physical and emotional elements. What is also obvious is that we tend to pay more attention to some needs than others—a fact which has about it a kernel of common sense.

In an understanding of human needs that has now come to be widely known and accepted, the psychologist Abraham Maslow organized them into a kind of hierarchy, with the meeting of basic needs for physical safety and well-being—for food, water, and shelter—providing the foundation for meeting other human needs.* Only after those are met, Maslow argued, can we deal with our needs for love and companionship, for acquisition of knowledge, and for a sense of identity and purpose.

That kind of approach is useful—up to a point. But we should be cautious on at least two counts. One is that this hierarchical arrangement of needs seems to neglect the fact that there are situations in which meeting the needs of the inner person are just as vital as meeting physical needs. In fact, meeting inner needs can sometimes *provide* a sense of safety.

As as extreme example, survivors of concentration camps sometimes testify to having been kept alive as much by hope, faith, and their attitude as by the meagre rations they were fed. And people with chronic illnesses may find laughter, love, companionship, and music as sustaining as the food they eat.

And the second thing we need to keep in mind here is that in our culture it is very easy to confuse needs with wants—especially in the material realm. Things considered needs by most of us in North America would be seen as luxuries in many other parts of the world.

I am not arguing in favor of neglecting basic physical needs. Meeting them is, and should be, a priority. Nor am I trying to make a case for subsistence living. I *am* suggesting, however, that some situations may require a perspective on our needs which is other than hierarchical. And that may sometimes be the case with crises having to do with employment.

Employment is directly and clearly related to meeting our basic needs. It earns us money, which in turn allows us to have food, shelter, and clothing. Providing for those needs often spills over into other areas as well. Having shelter and enough to eat, for example, clearly helps one's emotional well-being. And there is no question but that having our abilities and efforts rewarded monetarily helps us to feel good about ourselves.

So it is easy—and sometimes, even more respectable—to be primarily concerned with material things. We accept that it is important to do everything possible to provide ourselves with food, shelter, and clothing. But we are reluctant to deal with some of our other needs. We feel it is all right to express our needs for food and other things necessary for physical survival. But we are less willing to admit, even to ourselves, to needs having to do with love, meaning, or companionship, with the need to take time for exercise, for solitude, or for play.

In many cases, we deny those latter needs very well; we don't even let ourselves become consciously aware of them. If we do admit to them, we are likely to regard them as peripheral, or to believe that all of them can be met by way of more accomplishments, more luxuries, more material things. Or we may feel that they will be satisfied by having the right job, the right relationship, or sufficiently notable achievements.

Sometimes those tactics temporarily seem to succeed. But then, for one reason or another, we are challenged to look at life and ourselves in greater depth. We are called to attend to parts of ourselves we may have been neglecting or denying. We are called to make new discoveries, to engage more fully in the process of living, to begin a new phase of our journey. This is the call to give attention to the needs of the inner person as well as the outer one, to give attention to making a life, and it may well be precipitated by an employment crisis.

In order for us to live with integrity and authenticity and to build healthy self-esteem, we must we honor and value our inner needs as well as our outer ones. There is no question but that providing for food, shelter, and clothing is important. But it is also important to take seriously our inner needs: for love, for meaning, for affirmation of dignity and value beyond the bottom line.

Those needs are often associated with the spiritual realm of life, which can be understood in many different ways. Most often it is thought of in terms of our relationship with that which is transcendent, with a power that is greater than ourselves. In that framework, many people will think in terms of the beliefs, practices, and structures of organized religion.

But spirituality can also be understood in much broader terms—as openness to the infinite, as trust, awe, wonder, as recognition of the mystery of life and of the connectedness of all of life. And it can be seen, without any reference to a deity, as having to do with the struggle for meaning and identity in the context of our relationship with ourselves, with other human beings, and with the world around us. Understood in the most comprehensive way, spirituality has to do with concerns and struggles for meaning that go beyond immediate and material concerns.

One way of understanding spirituality, which can be useful to our discussion here, is to remember that we use the word "spirit" to suggest strength of life. To be a spirited person, for example, is to be a lively one. To be in good spirits suggests that one is reasonably happy and well.

And so it is that spirituality—or what could be called the "spirit factor" in life—can be understood as having to do with a wide range of things which activate and energize our spirits, and make us feel fully alive. Such things can include experiences as varied as prayer, worship, listening to music, reading a poem, gazing into the eyes of an infant, paddling a canoe on a quiet lake, or feeding grass to a docile mountain goat.

Both "soul" and "spirit," it seems to me, refer to dimensions of life other than surface ones. I sometimes think of "soul" as suggesting the dimension of depth. On the other hand, "spirit" seems to me to suggest the dimension of height, of reaching outward and upward, of connecting with an encompassing framework. Both words refer to those parts of our experience which hint at the timeless and the sacred.

Implicit in both soul and spirit—and creativity—is the notion of paradox—the notion that a thing or a happening cannot always be understood in either/or terms. To speak of paradox is to speak of the both/and nature of reality. It is to discover, for example, that a crisis sometimes turns out to be an opportunity which proves to be of value. It is the kind of viewpoint expressed by Ralph, the former seminar leader/business consultant, who spoke of his own crisis as having been a "good/bad thing."

As you know by now, a number of the people I interviewed saw the difficult parts of their experiences from a similar vantage point. In doing so, I suggest, they were adopting a stance that is essentially spiritual in nature—one which offers a larger-than-usual view of life experience. To see life in that sort of perspective is, in some sense, to be in touch with those parts of ourselves which, while not divorced from what we do for a living, are not dependent on it either.

In one way or another, all spiritual traditions remind us that human beings do not truly live by bread alone. Neither, of course, do we live by spirit alone. Which brings us back to the truth that our humanity is most fully understood not in terms of either/or but both/and. The challenge, in our culture anyway, is to avoid the tendency to neglect the emotional/spiritual in favor of the material, the commercial, and the monetary.

It is worth noting that some other cultures probably understand the importance of caring for the whole person better than we do. In some parts of the world, for example, it is not uncommon for people to do without certain basics in order to attend a cultural event. (I remember first becoming aware of that fact in a university course on music appreciation that I took. The professor was originally from Russia, and he spoke movingly of how it was not uncommon for people there to do without food in order to have enough money for the price of a ticket to the opera or the symphony.)

My point is simply that there is a perspective on life which goes beyond employment, beyond the marketplace, beyond any particular label or role. It takes into account our stories, our creativity, the ways in which we engage with our circumstances, the questions we ask as well as the answers we find, and with the things we care deeply about.

An employment crisis may awaken us to that kind of perspective. And if we are going to answer the call implicit in it, we need to take care of all of our needs, of our multidimensional self. Responding to life as effectively as possible, with as much power and creativity as possible, requires that we take care of our whole person.

I have already identified a number of elements involved in that kind of care: getting in touch with our stories and with our creativity, learning to interact with our experiences and challenges, and cultivating connectedness and community (both for the sake of finding and sharing strength and for that of finding purpose). Now I want to identify still other elements which can contribute to a healthy sense of self, with or without employment. The point to keep in mind is that our spiritual dimension, our inner person, can be accessed in many different ways.

We all know the truth of that fact; indeed, it is so obvious that we often overlook it. There are times, for instance, when we are worn out or bored, when we feel in a rut, when life seems flat and routine. And then we take time to do something a bit different. We work in the yard, we have a cup of tea, a friend calls or we call a friend, we walk through the woods, or do any of scores of other things, depending on our circumstances and tastes. Afterwards, we find ourselves feeling at least a little better. Things that may have been weighing upon us seem just a little less heavy.

There are various ways of explaining that kind of truth. But it seems to me that what happens is that we give one part of ourselves a rest and give a little nourishment to some of the other parts. To do so, of course, we have to make choices, and we have to give ourselves permission.

For some of us, the needs of the whole person become apparent only as a result of crisis—only when we are forced to confront them. For others, however, the awareness of those needs—and the importance of meeting them—is a more gradual thing.

One person whose story illustrates awareness of the importance of meeting all of her needs—and echoes some of the things I've been discussing—is a woman I'll call Beth, who started her professional work life as a nurse. She stayed with that career for about eight years, during which she met, married, and separated from her husband. For most of that time, she admitted, "the job was a means of income as well as a place to get some meaning." She said she was also "clear that I didn't want to get my identity from being a Mrs."

Beth's marriage ended only after efforts at reconciliation failed. Recalling that development, Beth told me, "I knew that he was not interested in continuing the marriage, and I let go. It was pain that I didn't want to experience because I knew there would be lots. But I knew that it was a turning point for me.

"I don't know just why I sensed that it was such a turning point. And I don't know why I've continued on the road I have, other than that there's been so many rewards for me and I'm fascinated in the change I see in myself and other people I work with."

That road has included therapy to deal with a number of issues in her life—issues having to do with food, with alcohol and tobacco, with having grown up in a family where there was alcoholism. And Beth went on to tell me about some other parts of her journey and the way in which she is caring for herself.

"I've done some intentional grieving around what I wasn't able to grieve when I was young...by which I mean I spent six months wearing black and doing some ritual things around my father's death. I've taken risks socially and in relationships that I wouldn't have before, and I've learned how to handle relationships better now that I've dealt with unfinished business from the past.

"I have a list of wants, or things I would like to do. What I'm doing now is I'm bike riding a lot. I love to do that, and I like to go places where it's peaceful and natural. I like to hike, I like to be active. But now I'm not approaching it the way I used to...like going four miles because I know it's going to burn off so many calories. And it's OK for me to miss a day. So the exercise is more healing now than it used to be.

"I quit watching TV over a year ago, and so I can use that time to read. And I'm becoming more interested in fiction, so that now when I put a book down I want to start another one, and that's not how it used to be. I still like going to movies but I'm picking ones that may not be commercially successful. I'm becoming more interested in European films.

"I love to be with my friends. I like to go swimming or do other physical things with them. I like to play baseball, or do spontaneous activities. I like to play darts and cards and scrabble. I like to listen to music. I like to be around animals; they give me lots of pleasure. If I'm on the street and see a person with a dog, I may stop and ask if I can pet it. So there are lots of things I can describe as being fun for me."

Another story which illustrates making choices and caring for the whole person is that of Glenn. A professional staff person with a major religious denomination until his recent retirement, Glenn found himself, some years ago, feeling a vague sense that something was missing from his life.

"I felt like I was really not doing anything for fun. It seemed like all I did was work at my job, work at church, and work at home. Being involved in church work as a profession, it seemed quite natural to be involved in it on Sundays as well. But I felt something was missing in my life, and for the sake of myself as well as my marriage I needed another interest.

"That kind of awareness was more cumulative than dramatic. But I did realize that as far as my marriage was concerned I was beginning to settle in and take a very unimaginative, uncreative approach to keeping it alive. We never really thought of separating, but there was something `dead' about it at the time. It came home to me one day when my wife returned from an appointment with a counselor she had been seeing and said, `Glenn, I want you to know that I stay with you not because I have to but because I choose to.' That was quite impressive to me. I had not much thought of doing anything else but staying together, but I realized that she had reached a real point of new growth herself. I became determined that I was going to try to do something that would enhance our lives.

"About that time we were invited to join two other couples on a three-day sailing trip. I was new to sailing, had never done much of anything outdoors, so I went along with the idea, but not with a lot of enthusiasm. But we spent three days and nights on the boat and I really enjoyed every minute of it.

"At the end of the three days, as I was getting off the boat, one of the people said, 'Glenn, you seem to have liked this experience. Now what are you going to do about it?' My response, which kind of surprised me, was that I would accept the next invitation to go sailing and start looking for a small boat to purchase. Which we did. And since then we've moved up several times to larger boats, and sailing has provided a tremendous dimension to my life.

"Pursuing this activity meant entering a new arena for me, discovering that there was a world out there of people who sail, just like there are people who play golf, there are people who take trips in Winnibagos, and so on. To enter the world of sailing was, for me, to begin to learn, to be involved in something new, which is exciting.

"And I realize I will never master the sport like some sailors do. But I don't have to do that in order to get the benefit of the outdoors, appreciation of all kinds of weather, and the recognition that there are some dangers involved. I guess one of the most significant discoveries I made as part of this experience was that if you are not willing to take a risk, you will never leave the dock.

"So I'm glad I left the dock. Somebody once said that the easiest time to accidentally flip a small boat over is when you're stepping into it. So it was a matter of taking that risk—not a big one, but a risk nevertheless.

"I believe I have grown spiritually through my sailing, in that I've had to venture out into new areas I was not familiar with. I have had to overcome fear to some degree. And sailing has caused me to feel a new sense of connectedness with my forebears, many of whom of course travelled by boat—not moving any faster than I did, but willing to go a great distance.

"I remember one time I was quite a distance off shore, at the helm of a rather large yacht. It was in the middle of the night, from 2:00 to 4:00 in the morning, and I remember thinking I had never realized how many stars there are in the sky. I was seeing them in a way I never had before. I don't think a person can do that without some feeling with and for God—or at least some feeling of awe."

Glenn's story is not intended to suggest that everyone should buy a sailboat. The point is simply that we do have choices, that life is more than bottom-line conformity, whatever its specific configuration. We need to give ourselves permission to exercise those choices in ways that are appropriate, responsible, and available to us.

Glenn, incidentally, is the husband of Moira, the teacher/counselor we met earlier. For her, as for many women, escaping an imposed role has meant engaging in job work. For Glenn, as for many men, it has meant detaching from that kind of work. The choices involved vary greatly from individual to individual. The important thing is that we make them in a conscious way.

We hear a good deal these days about the mind/body connection, with the focus often on the ways in which our minds can help us to heal and strengthen our bodies. And I would be the last to deny that truth. But sometimes we need to let our bodies lead the way in caring for the whole self. In somatic psychology, it is theorized that all of our emotions are encoded in our bodies. By taking care of our physical selves, we give the mind and spirit a chance to follow the body.

Activity that honors the body and the natural world was one of the most consistent elements in whole-person living for the people I talked with. We have just learned of that kind of commitment in Beth's and Glenn's lives. And Cheryl, the former architect, talked to me about having recently bought a kayak, and about being "very physical. I swim a lot...like every other day, or I play squash." And she added, "when I swim, I have a sense of well-being, which is really wonderful."

Sam, in spite of a heart condition, continues to travel regularly with his wife—which for them includes "backpacking and bumming around," often in Europe. Judith, the co-owner of the motorcycle shop, says she exercises regularly. Walking is very important for Brian, the former university administrator, and for Leon, who is now in forced retirement after spending most of his life as an accounts manager. Some years ago, Brad, the former corporate chemist, developed an interest in "the outdoors and hiking and wilderness trips" which continues to this day.

And there are many other readily available ways of strengthening the spirit by strengthening the body: dance, aerobic exercise, tennis, golf, jogging, skiing, and the oriental art known as Tai Chi, to name only a few. Almost any form of exercise can be beneficial to a person—although it is always advisable to use common sense and moderation in this matter, and to consult with your physician before engaging in strenuous activity.

Elements other than exercise are also involved in taking care of one's physical self. Good nutrition is a basic one, as more and more people are recognizing. And in the period just after his job termination, Brian found renewed vitality through therapeutic massage—which has been recognized for centuries as providing benefits for body, mind, and spirit.

Implicit in the notion of caring for the body is the avoidance of drugs, except when necessary and when prescribed by a physician, avoidance of nicotine, and abstinence or moderation in the use of alcohol.

One helpful technique that encompasses the body and more is meditation, which, contrary to the beliefs of some, is not limited to those who adhere to eastern religions or to New Age beliefs. In fact, one does not have to be at all "religious" to meditate, and in recent years the practice has begun to enter the mainstream of western culture. The reason is simple: meditation is a very practical and beneficial resource for living.

It can be very helpful in dealing with stress, for example.

Taking even a short time to calm the mind and pay attention to our breathing—which is at the core of meditation—can be a way of accessing the sense of inner control which I spoke of earlier as being at the heart of dealing effectively with stress. Taking time to access that sense of control—even briefly—can help us to feel less threatened by those many parts of life which are clearly beyond our control. It can help us to meet life as openly and as wholeheartedly as possible.

Meditation, says Jon Kabat-Zinn, Director of the Stress Reduction Program at the University of Massachusetts Medical School, is a way of practicing "non-doing," a way of practicing "being." It is, he goes on to say, "really about paying attention."* And Lawrence LeShan, writing in his little book *How to Meditate,* says that "we meditate to find, to recover, to come back to something of ourselves we once dimly and unknowingly had and have lost without knowing what it was or when we lost it."* In that connection he quotes a man who attended one of his workshops as saying that meditation is "like coming home."

It is beyond the scope of our discussion here to go into detail concerning the practice of meditation. If you wish to explore the matter in depth, you would be well advised to consult other resources. By way of introducing the subject, however, I should mention that there there is no one way of meditation that is "right" for everyone. It can be very brief and informal or quite lengthy and require a great deal of discipline. The basic requirement is a bit of time and silence. And the basic guidelines are that you be aware of the present moment and that you be conscious—or mindful—of your breathing.

One value of concentrating on our breathing is that doing so reminds us that we actually do our living—and our breathing—in the present. We cannot breathe for tomorrow; we can only breathe for now. And thus it is that *whatever else we are, we are our breathing.*

So pay attention to your inhaling and your exhaling. As you do so, you will undoubtedly become aware of distracting thoughts. Usually it is best to acknowledge them and then send them on their way, knowing that you can attend to them later. Stay with the present; stay with your breathing.

Ideally, meditation is done on a regular basis, preferably once or twice a day, for at least ten to fifteen minutes. It is best to assume a comfortable position, with spine straight and feet on the floor. Wear comfortable clothing. Breathe in and out, slowly and naturally, preferably through your diaphragm—through your belly rather than your chest. Some people find it helpful to repeat a word or a simple phrase or to count slowly, with each breath, from one to five. But the key thing is to focus on your breathing and to adopt a receptive attitude.

By doing these things we can get in touch with our bodies and our minds. We can become more fully conscious and more open to insights and awareness that come from a level below consciousness. Meditation is a way of reconnecting with vital parts of ourselves that too often get lost in our strivings. It is a way of listening to the "still small voice" inside each of us.

For some, paying attention to that "still small voice" may be understood in the framework of organized religion and faith. I have talked about spirituality in generic terms, primarily as a dimension of life, but faith and religion are ways in which many of us know spirituality in a more formal, credal way. For those who find spirituality in such a context, it surely needs to be understood as potentially beneficial for whole-person living. Prayer, worship, study of sacred texts, a caring community of faith, and trust in a loving deity can be vital resources. They warrant our respect even if we choose not to make use of them.

Taking care of our whole person also means taking some time apart from our usual activities to attend to things previously ignored—including little things. And taking time apart also has to do with boundaries—including those we may need to erect to protect ourselves from too much busyness, which can be a part of the job search process as well as of job work itself.

Although we need connectedness with others, we also need

time alone—time for solitude. This need can be met in many ways, but it again comes back to choices. For example, Brad finds solitude in his hiking and backpacking, Cheryl finds it in her kayak, Glenn finds it on his sailboat. Taking time for those things doesn't happen automatically; it doesn't happen by default.

Keith, the civil servant I briefly introduced earlier, the one who has a reputation for being easy to talk to, travels a good deal in connection with projects he is responsible for overseeing. Much of his travelling is by car in rural areas. He talked to me about the way he tries to arrange his schedule. "I'll give myself some extra time to get there...take a less travelled road...stop at a roadside park or just at the side of the road and look around... see a deer, stop and watch it. I'm able to do that. I can stop and smell the roses."

What he is talking about brings me to another suggestion, namely the importance of doing nothing at times. In a sense, of course, meditating is doing nothing—in Jon Kabat-Zinn's terminology, it is practicing "non-doing." And it's valuable to do that in a regular, structured way if we're so inclined. But it's also important to make room in our lives for doing nothing just for the sake of doing nothing.

Most of us, however, tend to be much better at *doing* than at *not-doing*. We can sympathize with Judith, who took a year off after leaving her corporate position and discovered that she "didn't know how to do nothing." It was something she had to learn—and it wasn't easy.

We are sometimes reminded that not working can be very productive. We often make valuable discoveries just when we least expect them. We work hard at something, only to feel that the answer is further away than ever. Then we give up, surrender to the moment, and suddenly, "Eureka!"—we have the insight that provides clarity and allows us to move forward.

Caring for the whole person, for ourselves off the job as well as on the job, means allowing for the "Eureka!" moments—the "Aha!" moments. It means being aware that we can sometimes work too hard, and that doing so can be counterproductive. *Of even greater importance, it means understanding that not only our productivity but our well-being can be fostered by taking time to do nothing, that our true work sometimes means not working.*

Our real work also includes living mindfully—which is closely related to meditation, but on an ongoing basis. Being mindful means attending to the present moment. It is a kind of meditation in action. It means paying attention to what we are doing—whether it's the laundry, eating, gazing at flowers, making love, or making the bed.

That kind of "in-the-momentness" is in sharp contrast to the way in which most of us live most of the time. Usually, we are doing one thing while thinking about another. Mindfulness means being open to the possibility that there may be significance, strength, and benefit to be found in the present moment, even if there is pain involved in it. It is to be open to the possibility that what is happening *now* may have more to offer than we at first thought.

To speak of the importance of the present, of non-doing, and of taking time for activities we normally term "nonproductive" brings us to an obviously related topic—namely, the importance of play. Like the word "work," the word "play" is subject to a number of different connotations in the English language. For example, we can play with a kitten, we can play tennis, and, if we are so talented, we can play the piano.

The first example most clearly resembles the kind of play I want to discuss here. In that sense, in the words of author Stephen Nachmanovitch, play is "the free spirit of exploration, doing and being for its own pure joy."* And the authors of *Chop Wood, Carry Water,* a book about spirituality in everyday life, speak of it as being "something wonderfully free and aimless, the spark that makes life worth living."* It can be a wonderful way of "letting off steam," a valuable antidote to the stresses and challenges of living, including those associated with the world of job work.

Many of us, unfortunately, are not very good at playing in that way. We are probably better at playing games. Games are played according to rules; games allow one to *work* at something—one's backhand or one's putting, for example. In that framework, moreover, playing is often thought to require the right equipment or the correct clothing. According to many messages we are sent these days, one does not play in just any clothes or with just any equipment. It must be quite correct—and often quite expensive. Like so much of what we do in our culture, play has become a very businesslike affair.

But play in the sense I am talking about here is an attitude as much as an activity, a way of approaching things rather than any particular thing. And it is that kind of attitude—akin to the "letting go" involved in creativity, which gets us in touch with parts of ourselves which we often neglect. To know how to play is to be in touch with the child within us. It is to help bring to life our total self, our true self.

A healthy sense of humor goes hand in hand with play. Humor is another resource whose benefits to well-being are getting overdue attention. One person who helped make us aware of the benefits of humor was author Norman Cousins, who some years ago was afflicted with a life-threatening degenerative condition of his spinal column. Discovering that a good belly laugh significantly reduced his need for pain-killing drugs, he persuaded his doctors to include in his treatment regular screenings of old movies that would make him laugh.

Cousins, as you may know, recovered from his illness, lived many more years, and wrote about the therapeutic value of laughter in his recovery*—an assessment with which his doctors agreed. In the years since then, the benefits of humor and laughter have been extolled more and more—both as they relate to serious health issues and to general well-being.

No one is suggesting, of course, that humor is some kind of magic wand for making problems disappear. But there is evidence that it can have both psychological and physiological benefits. Whatever else it may do, laughter can help us to let go of our concerns, even if only momentarily. A good belly laugh can help to recharge us. Learning to laugh at ourselves helps us to get outside ourselves—which, paradoxically, can help us to connect with the deeper parts of ourselves.

One way our sense of humor is often nourished is by being with other people and sharing stories. Humor almost invariably sneaks in any time people share their common humanity. And comedy is available through movies and television—and the comic strips in the daily newspapers. Such resources are readily available and can contribute much to well-being. They can confirm the vantage point offered by the late comedian Grady Nutt, who often said that "laughter is the hand of God on the shoulders of a troubled world."

We also care for our whole person through the strength and power of art, music, and words. Here I have in mind both appreciation and expression. That is, we can nourish ourselves both by viewing art and by doing it, both by listening to music and by playing it, both by reading and by writing. We do not have to become professionals in any of those areas—though I surely would not want to rule out that possibility for persons who have the talent. The point is that we all have the ability to respond to music, art and writing, and to express ourselves in those ways. To fail to be open to that truth is to do ourselves a disservice.

There are, of course, various forms of writing—from letters to business proposals, from poetry to novels to drama and screenplays. The emphasis here, however, is not on any particular form, but on putting one's thoughts, insights, concerns, fears and the like down on paper. For we are increasingly coming to understand that expressing one's self through the written word, whatever its form, can be beneficial to well-being.

For example, writing consultant and teacher Gabriele Rico argues that "by externalizing feelings in words, we gain a greater ability to take charge of our own lives, and begin to see the patterns within the seeming chaos."* And that kind of truth is also articulated by a psychologist by the name of James Pennebaker, who for some years has emphasized the connection between writing and wellness and who recently completed a study which suggests that expressing your feelings in writing may actually help in the job search process.* The explanation, according to one report on the study, is that writing helps people to deal with their emotions and to reappraise their situations, and that they are therefore able to present themselves better in job interviews.

The form of writing which may be the one most commonly recommended for encouraging well-being is the keeping of a journal. The word "journal" itself, of course, suggests a record of a journey and, as such, a journal can be very helpful as an unfolding account of how we respond to our experiences. Having that kind of record is not likely to provide us with solutions to our problems. But it can help us to understand and appreciate the questions that we bring to our unfolding experience.

But whatever writing we do—whether it is a journal, a short story, poetry, random jottings, or something else—what is important is to allow ourselves to experiment with the use of words, and to be open to the insights, strength, and healing that can come from the process.

Many people are probably more than a little reluctant to try writing a short story or poetry. But if the slightest inclination is there, there is no reason not to pursue it. Children write stories all the time and one of the values of writing—of creativity of any sort—is that it helps us to get in touch with the child within each of us, with the part of us willing to experiment, to improvise, and to play. And the same thing is true of poetry. There is ample evidence that people of all ages, from all backgrounds and walks of life, can learn to put words together poetically and that their lives are strengthened and enriched by doing so.

The other side of self-expression through writing is reading—benefitting from the writing of others. And never has there been such an array of books from which to choose. There are, for example, many titles having to do with unemployment and other job-related matters. If such issues are of concern to you, you may want to search out and make use of resources having to do with that subject. In addition, as even a cursory glance through any bookstore will confirm, there are self-help books available on virtually every conceivable topic. Many of those volumes are also available in libraries.

In addition to nonfiction, there is also the world of fiction, which brings us back to the importance of stories as a source of strength and power. While sharing our stories in person is desirable, it is not the only way to discover the power of story.

Reading fiction, and listening to our heart, mind, and soul as we do so, is a way of getting in touch with and affirming our own stories. As Joseph Gold, author of *Read For Your Life,* reminds us, "Fiction helps us to rewrite our stories, helps us to revise, review and add on stories, so that we can continue living our narrative in a creative way."* And biography offers similar benefits. In either case, we learn about ourselves by relating to others through the written word.

And, finally, no discussion of the benefits and power of words would be complete without a reference to reading poetry. (I do not want to try to define that word, but suffice it to say that it involves using language for maximum impact in depth. As such, it can resonate with many dimensions of our being.) In the words of psychologist Mihaly Csikszentmihalyi, "Reading from a book of poems each night is to the mind [and soul and spirit] as working out on a Nautilus is to the body—a way for staying in shape."* It is not essential that the poetry be great—or even that poems be read in their entirety. Even one word, Csikszentmihalyi reminds us, may open the way to a new and expanding inner journey of discovery.

I have spent a good deal of time talking about ways in which words can help to strengthen and nourish us, in part because of their ready availability. But the same general benefits can also be obtained from two other forms of creative expression—art and music.

While it may be true that not everyone can perform music, it is the case that anyone can draw and paint, that anyone can learn to respond to the artwork of others, and that anyone can be moved by music. And part of the advantage of those forms of expression is that they are somewhat different from that which is routine for most of us.

Visual art, for example, has to do primarily with the right side of the brain, the side which has to do with spatial thinking and perception. The left side of the brain, which is the one used more frequently in daily living and working, has to do with logical, sequential processing of data.

Of course, we all use both sides of the brain all the time, but it is the left side that is dominant for most of us in most situations. Visual art, therefore, whether we create it or simply enjoy it, calls upon a part of us which does not get that much use. And calling upon that neglected part can be energizing and a boon to the human spirit.

I have become more conscious of that fact in recent years as I have dared to venture a bit from the world of words, which is one I know reasonably well, into the world of art classes. I am confident that no professional artists are going to be threatened by my talent in any way. But that fact is part of the pleasure I get from exploring it. For I have been able to do it simply as something pleasurable for its own sake. Although I try to develop whatever skill I possess, I have been rather blissfully indifferent to the quality of the end result—which, I suspect, has probably improved it.

And while I am not a musician, I can hardly imagine life without music. I listen to it regularly—classical, folk, some country western—especially as I drive. Sometimes I deliberately choose to play a tape rather than listen to the news—as a reminder, for me, of a level of reality that is deeper and more lasting than the latest crisis and the most recent economic and political pronouncements.

My reason for outlining these resources is that, whatever else they do, they help us to transcend—and transform—immediate concerns. They take us beyond the toxicity and banality that too often are the major parts of what we feed upon. By doing so, they help us to get a fresh perspective on ourselves and on our circumstances. They remind us of the "forest" when we are obsessed with the "trees" of the moment.

Keep in mind that psychological creativity and the creativity associated with talent are not mutually exclusive. Exposing ourselves to expressions of creativity and allowing ourselves to make our own expressions are both ways of nourishing our inner creativity, which is an integral part of our true selves.

We need to give ourselves permission not only to view life creatively but to nurture whatever talent and special interests we have. We sometimes think that all truly talented people are able to pursue their creative bent full-time and that, if we cannot pursue ours full-time, there is no point in pursuing it.

But there are countless examples which suggest otherwise. Anton Chekhov, for example, was a physician as well as being a short story writer and playwright. (He is said to have remarked that medicine was his lawful wedded wife and literature was his mistress—and that when he tired of one he spent time with the other.) William Carlos Williams was also a physician—and a poet. T. S. Eliot worked for many years as a bank clerk, all the while writing poetry. Nathaniel Hawthorne and Franz Kafka were novelists who respectively worked in a customs house and as a government clerk; the poet Robert Frost was a farmer for many years; Wallace Stevens was an insurance executive as well as a poet.

And the list need not be limited to those whose abilities are well known. Earlier I mentioned an artist and an actor, each of whom has made at least part of his living from endeavors other than his primary creative commitment. And I also can think of a businessman in Pennsylvania, and a teacher and a doctor in Winnipeg, who are all potters. A New York newspaperman I once knew used to make exquisite jewelry, and I know a dentist who plays in a jazz band and a psychologist who is a published poet. Leon, the former accounts manager we met earlier, now finds time for woodworking, stamp collecting, and reading; Brian, the former university administrator, spends a good deal of time working on his family's genealogy. And my list could go on and on. Many of you could undoubtedly make a much longer one, either from your own experience or that of someone else.

We often dismiss creative activities by saying that they are merely hobbies. We use the word "amateur" to suggest nothing more than second class quality and, if we develop a number of talents or interests, we may be inclined to label ourselves as dilettantes.

Yet the fact is that an amateur is literally one who does something out of love, and a dilettante is one who takes delight in a subject or activity. So, by disdaining those words, we have simply bought into the popular viewpoint that only that which has commercial value is important. But the truth is that you don't have to be a professional in order to be an artist—in order to express yourself creatively.

As we've discussed, part of the challenge of living is to discover ways of nourishing wholeness in ourselves. And we do so by taking time to do the things that matter to us, the things we do simply for the sake of doing them, the things in which we both lose ourselves and find a new and stronger sense of who we are.

We would like to think that our employment offers those kinds of activities. And in some cases, it does—or did. But for a lot of people it doesn't. And if we are going to feel good about ourselves, if we are going to find the strength we need to meet both personal and social challenges, we need to pay attention to those activities that are beneficial to our well-being and that make us feel good about ourselves, whether or not we get paid for them. We need to give ourselves permission to take seriously those things which bring us joy and hope, which help us to savor and to celebrate life.

One of the best ways I know of for dealing with frustrations related to job work—whether we're talking about unemployment, retirement, or putting up with a job that is unsatisfying—is to take time for things that are creative and energizing. To do so is to nourish our souls and to re-equip ourselves for facing the difficult parts of the journey.

It all comes back to the importance of seeing work in its true light—which may well be different from the way we usually see it. It may be that the work we do "on the side" is more complementary to our growth than is the work we do for someone else's bottom line. It may be that we need to resurrect to new respectability the now seldom-used notion of avocation.

However we understand it, the important thing is to remember that taking time for whatever creative bent we have—whether or not it has to do with a specific talent—is to claim an asset of inestimable value to our self-esteem and our self-actualization. Taking time for what we care about, taking time to nourish parts of ourselves that tend to be neglected by the job work world to which we must conform to some degree, is a way of valuing ourselves without excessive dependency on that world's approval.

This is not to say we need to abandon standard values. It is simply to suggest that instead of being tied exclusively to the standard ones, we can develop values of our own and choose ways of affirming them and ourselves. And part of doing so lies in learning to enjoy and find meaning in the process of living itself. It lies in discovering and savoring whatever is good and empowering in the present as an antidote to the tendency too many of us have to live primarily for the future.

One thing crucial to achieving that objective is a commitment to lifelong learning, which was a common denominator in the way in which all of the people I interviewed now approach their lives. I have already mentioned the fact that Moira, in retirement, is taking a university course. Some years ago her husband, Glenn, made a New Year's resolution to read one book a month that year. He kept that resolution. And reading a book a month—on a wide variety of subjects, fiction and nonfiction—simply became part of his life. Brad, too, is a committed reader—and not just in the field of science.

What these examples illustrate is that personal growth can be a lifelong affair. It does not stop at age 21 or 55 or 75, or at any age. As long as we are alive there will be new information to be gathered, new curiosities to be explored regarding the the world in which we live, ourselves and our potential, and our sense of purpose and meaning. And the fortunate thing, in the words of an oft-quoted adage, is that when the "student" is ready, the "teacher" does in fact appear—whether in the form of a person, a group of people, circumstances, or a combination thereof.

I have given a great deal of attention in this chapter to the importance of taking time for yourself, for the things that energize you and develop wholeness. But I would be remiss if I did not emphasize again that we are not islands unto ourselves and that an integral part of taking care of and affirming ourselves includes taking time for others. We sometimes find ourselves by forgetting ourselves.

One word that comes to mind as I think about the matters I have discussed in this chapter is "balance." It is a word which can suggest a number of things, including balance between body, mind, and spirit, and between our personal, professional, and social lives. For some of us, however, it may seem to suggest blandness, lack of passion and commitment, or being well-adjusted to the point of apathy.

But balance can be healing. It is an integral part of medicine as it is practiced in many parts of the world. It is of benefit in dealing with stress. It is an antidote to obsession. And balance can also contribute to energy and vitality. Stephen Nachmanovitch, the philosopher and author I've cited several times, uses riding a bicycle as an example—explaining that balance means "continuous adjustment of continuous change."*

Balance, therefore, is closely linked to creativity and to caring about and attending to the present in a spirit of surrender. And the bike riding metaphor can serve to remind us that living fully, with enthusiasm, is a total experience—involving body, mind, heart, ego, spirit, soul, right brain and left brain, joy, sadness, paradox, shadow, and more.

Implicit in that reminder is the truth that approaching life in a way that incorporates the whole person is to know a fulfillment which is not possible by trying to meet all of our needs by obsessive attachment to one outlet, activity, or identity. It brings us back to the fact that self-discovery is a journey, and to the need to think further about how we might respond to that reality.

Chapter Seven

JOBS, WORK, AND THE SOJOURNER STANCE

We live out our lives in the midst of paradox. There are many elements that are part of our experience which seem contradictory, at least at one level. To cite an example pertinent to us here, we all have a desire for permanence on the one hand and for change on the other. We long for both stability and for variety. We want to be secure, but we don't want to get stuck in a rut.

Our attachment to our job work—and to the sense of identity we derive from it—grows out of our desire for that which is fixed and unchanging. That desire can be seen even in the midst of career mobility. Even if our occupation involves movement—either geographic or career—it is nevertheless an *occupation.* The word itself, as I pointed out earlier, is a variation of the verb "to occupy"—i.e., to hold a place.

North America has a heritage of movement and of change. The people who brought European ways to North America—for good or for ill—were people who were restless, who had been uprooted either by choice or, in many cases, by necessity.

Yet our popular mythology also includes the image of the dedicated company person—the one who stays with the same firm for a number of decades and retires with a gold watch. And although we may sense the passing of that kind of option, we cling to it—or at least to some variation which offers a similar kind of security.

Our desire for stability has been heightened by our having grown accustomed to more affluent lifestyles and their accompanying expenses: mortgages, car loans, tuition and the like. As well as wanting the income that allows us to enjoy such things, we want the pension and insurance benefits that go with many jobs and that many people have come to expect.

Most of us, moreover, have lived our lives in the shadow—and I use the word advisedly—of the notion of progress. In our culture, that notion means that bigger is better and that the only meaningful mobility is that which is upward. In job work terms, this translates into understanding success as having as much money and security as possible. Many of us are quite willing to accept changes, provided they mean raises and promotions.

Our desire to fix our identity in terms of our job work is closely intertwined with all of these factors. We want to feel that we are "in place," that we have a position of security and, perhaps, even comfort. And we tend to understand place in terms of material benefits. If we have to leave one place, we like to think that it will be for another one that is in some sense better. We may admire risk takers, but most of us are not programmed to take risks.

And, of course, we have a special aversion to risk and vulnerability that are foisted on us by people or circumstances over which we have no control. Sometimes we go to extreme lengths to avoid that kind of risk—for example, by looking for a new job even while we are reasonably happy in our present one.

Yet the fact is that life repeatedly confronts us with the need to change, with the need to let go and move on. In one fashion or another we are repeatedly driven from the place we have occupied. As history professors are fond of reminding their students, nothing is constant but change. That truth is operative for nations, for cultures, for organizations, and for individuals.

And it is through change, including change involving loss, that we grow. As Judith Viorst reminds us in her book *Necessary Losses*, life begins with loss.* We all begin our journey by leaving a secure environment—our mother's womb—and entering a world that is less secure but more exciting. And, in countless ways throughout our lives, the process repeats itself. We let go of childhood, we let go of adolescence, we let go of parents. And in the process, we take hold of new ways and new roles. We occupy new positions, one of which almost invariably has to do with our job work or its equivalent. And we understandably attach special importance to that one. Unfortunately, we often attach ourselves and our whole identity as a valuable human being to it.

As many people are discovering, however, that attachment can be very tenuous. It can, in fact, be broken—often when we least expect it and are least prepared for it. When this happens, we may be left feeling that we have lost not only our employment but also our sense of who we are. Throughout this book I have tried to suggest approaches to living and working which can help us to be less dependent on job work for our self-esteem and sense of identity. Underlying everything I have said is the conviction that job work is only *part* of one's real work, and that the latter consists of participating as fully and creatively as possible in life and engaging in the process of realizing our potential.

Now I want to propose a stance toward living and working which is consistent with all of those other suggestions. It is the stance suggested by the word "sojourner." To sojourn is to occupy a place, but for a limited period of time. It is to see the place one has as a kind of way station—important, to be sure, but part of the larger journey. The concept of sojourning encompasses the paradox inherent in our desire for both rootedness and change. As such, it can be a useful metaphor for our occupational identity.

The word "sojourner" is not one that is heard much these days. The reason may be that it runs counter to values which are dominant in our culture, such as position, status, security, and obsession with occupation. And we like to think of occupation—and of identity by way of occupation—as something fixed and secure. It is something to be achieved and held. In keeping with those values, occupation is often thought of in terms of competition, even conquest.

Our immigrant ancestors no doubt understood the nature of sojourning far better than we do. They accepted the tenuousness of life as a matter of course. To be sure, they sought security—in hearth, home, and occupation. But the kind of security and comfort that we tend to take for granted was simply unknown to most of them.

Again, I am not arguing for subsistence living. But I cannot help but think that the standard of living which many of us have come to think of as our right may lead us toward a perspective on life that is a bit out of focus. It may make us prone to view that which is material and thus seemingly secure as being all there is to life. And so it is that we may be made exceptionally uncomfortable when we find ourselves "in transit," stuck in circumstances which arouse in us more than a little anxiety.

To be a sojourner is not to be indifferent to one's employment needs or to one's surroundings and responsibilities in general. But it is to see things in perspective. It is to wear one's "occupational identity" garments loosely. It is to be more concerned with spirit, soul, and selfhood in depth than with ego. It is therefore to be a sign of wholeness and hope.

We may need to shift toward the model of living and working that is suggested by the word sojourner. That model encompasses the desire for rootedness and the reality of change—both the desire for stability and acceptance of the transience of life. It can encourage us to participate creatively and responsibly in the present while at the same time being open to new experience and the need for change. It recognizes that life is not static but dynamic and it allows for the fact that movement and growth can be interior as well as exterior—and, moreover, that exterior movement doesn't have to be upward in order to be significant.

To approach life and one's identity as a sojourner is to approach job work more in terms of stewardship than of ownership. To be a steward, as I am using the word, is to hold something in trust. It is not incompatible with ownership. We can "own" our lives and talents, even while seeing them as gifts we have been entrusted with. Stewardship refers to a perspective on life and work. To be a good steward is to recognize the importance of responsibility in the midst of transience, that what we "own" is ours to care for, but for a limited time. An appropriate metaphor might be tending a vineyard rather than building an empire.

The sojourner stance does not rule out putting down roots. In fact, it recognizes that putting down roots is very important. But it is also consistent with keeping life as simple as possible, and with keeping our wants and desires within limits. Too often we let those wants and desires get out of hand and overextend our resources—sometimes in an attempt to establish our identity. To do so is often to add to the stress of life, especially when the unexpected happens.

To see oneself as a sojourner is to recognize that life is not a group of isolated transitions but that it is in fact an ongoing transition—broken, to be sure, by plateaus, by resting places, by oases, but nonetheless an ongoing journey, of which job work is but a part. It is to realize that identity is not a role one occupies. Rather, it is through engaging with life on our journey that we call forth an identity—not as something to be labeled but as an awareness to be experienced.

And it may well be that our identity is called forth not so much on the broad freeways of life as on its narrow, bumpy detours—not so much from exulting in our successes as from learning to sing in the midst of our setbacks. As Ernest Kurtz puts it in his book, *The Spirituality of Imperfection*, "Identity captures us, overtaking us especially in moments of pain and anguish—when we are lost and searching, stumbling and falling."*

Which brings us back once again to Odysseus—the political leader and general, the warrior who was good at winning battles. But then he lost one which should have been a sure win. And what was supposed to have been a short trip home to a hero's welcome turned out to be a tortuous journey of many years, which the author of *The Odyssey* has him recount as a way of identifying himself.

And so it is with most of us. We cling to our labels, to our one-dimensional identity as long as possible. But then our complacency is interrupted; we are jolted out of our comfortable routines. It may happen in connection with a health crisis, the breakup of a marriage or other intimate relationship, "hitting bottom" in the course of alcoholism or some other addiction, or, as for many of us, an employment crisis. But it may also be experienced simply as a deep dissatisfaction with living a surface existence. Whatever the particulars, we are forced to let go of the notion of a "fixed" identity and become open to a deeper awareness of who we are.

To commit ourselves to that openness is to take seriously the place we occupy but also to recognize that it is ours only for a time; it is not who we are. We therefore broaden our perspective. We refuse to be too attached to our image, refuse to be overly concerned about matters of ego concerns. We recognize that we find our identity in our journey, not in our labels, and that although we have an identity, it is continuing to unfold. We are who we are, but we are also who we are becoming.

What I am terming the sojourner stance was implicit in the stories of all those I interviewed for this book. Often their stories also illustrate the notion of identity as a lifelong process of discovery. For example, you may remember Beth—the nurse whose divorce was a turning point in her life, one that was painful but that set her on a new route.

Although she was still working as a nurse when we talked, Beth was moving toward getting a degree as an expressive arts therapist, a decision which has grown out of her struggles: "I think I have some of my skills because of the pain that I had. I didn't recognize that at the time, but now I'm feeling fortunate that I've had that kind of experience."

And there have been other interesting developments in her life. For example, the school she attended had what was termed a "Paris semester," and Beth was able to spend part of a year in France. "I think one of my reasons the experience did so much for me was that I decided to live in another culture, putting myself in a situation that I knew would be difficult for me, but also looking for some excitement and some adventure. I'm interested in the arts, and I decided Paris would be a good place to be. And I also liked the idea of dating French men."

At the time of our interview Beth was making plans for a second visit to Scotland, where she is from originally. She went there following her semester in France to visit her grandmother and decided to make another trip for the grandmother's 90th birthday.

"My job is flexible, so I can go back to Scotland to do some healing for myself and be available to my grandmother. She would never ask for the visit, but she's excited that I'm coming. And also I'm going back to Sinhorn [a retreat in Scotland] to do some workshops and to be in a community where I can get some of my needs met by sharing feelings with some other people."

She also has become aware of a correlation between her connectedness with other people and the strength she finds. She talked about the importance of "having people in my life who will encourage me and be there for me even when I'm doing scary things...so that I don't stop or avoid doing something because it's scary...like going to Paris."

Beth admitted that she could easily become "attached" to the therapist label. But she was confident that her priority would remain her own development. "It's like the more I find out about myself, the more awareness I have. The more I change behaviors that I don't like, the more I'm available to other people.

"I know that my work is around letting go. It's about not being controlling, which continually comes up in my life. It's about accepting people the way they are, not asking them to be different. It's about knowing my agenda versus their agenda. It's about loving and being in the present."

And, as she reflected further, she talked again about the importance of her network of friends. "I have people in my life who accept me for where I am, so that when I get into a place of wanting to be somewhere else or someone else, they accept that I'm continually in transition, continually changing, and they will say to me that they love me the way I am."

As I think of the sojourning stance, I am also reminded of Sam, who decided to back away from what had been an obsession with corporate-based status and is now helping friends and neighbors learn to do their own home repairs and being a support person for individuals with AIDS and their families.

And there was Brad, whose career movement has been from the corporate world to teaching in a small college, and Norman, who moved from the business world to claim his own priorities as a photographer. There was also Cheryl, the architect who went from an identity based on competition to one which affirms the importance of community.

Judith, you may remember, left an upwardly-mobile career track with a major corporation and moved to a different state. For a year she forced herself to do nothing—which she felt was important to her. And she subsequently became the co-owner of a motorcycle shop—a job which lets her be active in supporting the social concerns that are important to her.

There was Glenn, whose decision to buy a sailboat led him to "cast off" in more ways than one, and Moira, whose journey led her to discard many of her inherited myths about being a wife and mother, to move beyond the social identity that had been assigned to her, and to pursue a retirement which promises to be full and creative.

We met Eric and Lisa, who are struggling to balance the standardized world of job work with ways of living and working which honor their relationship, their individual priorities, and their desire to contribute to the wider community.

And you may remember Keith, the civil servant who is known for being easy to talk to. Keith's sojourn has included a number of jobs, and an extended period as a househusband. Speaking of the latter experience, he recalled, "I didn't find it that difficult. I did stuff around the house. I cooked, I did some wash, I did a bit of cleaning, I was there for the kids when they came home from school, and to drive them places. I tried to help my wife in different ways. She was working full-time."

Keith also sees that period of his life as a time of useful discovery and preparation. "I learned that I have a really good imagination and that I could come up with unique ideas and unique solutions to things. I learned that you don't have to follow recipes to make good soup."

It's a discovery that he feels serves him well in the job that he now has. As he put it during our interview, "the more unusual the situation is that I have to work with, the harder I work to find a solution."

During his unemployment Keith also did a good deal of volunteer work, which is proving to be another plus. "Most of the people I deal with are volunteers and, because of my own experience, I can understand their point of view better than many people in positions similar to mine."

Like many of the people I talked with, Keith views success in terms of "enjoying what you're doing." And he includes in its parameters his relationship with his wife and four daughters: "I think I'm more successful today because of the relationship I have with my wife and kids. And if I had to choose between my job and those relationships, I would choose the latter. I'm not saying it would be easy, but I would work it out because the relationships would be more important."

We also met Peter, who lost his job as a journalist and had to give up his ideas about the importance of being *the* breadwinner of the family. In the course of coming to terms with that change he experienced a time of depression. But he gained new awareness of himself and appreciation for the simple things of life—a smile from a stranger, having potatoes to eat.

And there was Ted, who for years made use of all of the recommended job search strategies to no avail, only to find a position in the human resource field when he was at the point of giving up his search.

Leon and Brian have both discovered that there is life after retirement—even though it came a bit sooner than they might have expected. Leon, you may recall, lost his job as the result of a corporate merger. For Brian, the loss came at the end of more than two decades as a university administrator. Both spoke of having found a deeper sense of identity and new joy in living.

At the other end of the career spectrum, Richard is the recent Ph.D. graduate who has had to detach from being overly concerned about his career even before getting settled into one. He is using the experience as a kind of field test for some of his theories about creativity and problem solving.

Ralph is the former seminar leader and business consultant who was brought up short by a health crisis. It reminded him of the transience of life and of the importance of taking time for his family and for himself.

Frank is the former school teacher we met who, in the course of a very difficult transition period, had a dream which led him to embrace his uniqueness and gave him a new perspective on his career. He now sees his job work as only part of his life—as what he does for a living rather than as the sole definition of who he is.

And you may remember that Norman, after decades of relegating his creative bent to the sidelines, is now exploring his interests and abilities as a professional photographer. As well, he is learning to trust and to feel, to view his life as a whole as a way of expressing his creativity.

In addition, there are three other sojourners I would like for you to meet. One is Derek, who is currently an oncologist specializing in work with the terminally ill. But his employment history includes work in the computer field and for an oil company in the Middle East.

Derek takes his responsibilities as a physician seriously. He is, however, a seeker by nature, and he speculates that he might yet pursue study and a career in something other than clinical medicine—perhaps psychology or one of the other helping professions.

Now in his early 40s, he acknowledged that he makes a good income, but he also told me, without apparent concern, that "I have earned less money every year since I left university at 21 or 22." He added that "if I decide to stop working as an oncologist and do something else, I could probably do it. But if I switched again, I'd never make it to any pinnacle of that profession; there wouldn't be enough time. I would do it because that's what I wanted to do, because something inside of me said, 'yes that's what I ought to be doing.'

"I cannot yet see the impetus to organize my life's goals in order to be able to retire. I cannot accept that it isn't more important, to use Joseph Campbell's words, `to follow your bliss,' than it is to worry about whether there's going to be money for retirement. I'm curious about what I'll be doing in 20 years, but I'm not fixated on it. I don't really know, and I'm prepared to wait and see."

He also told me that "the process of going without any money for some years through medical school helped my wife and me to clarify many of our objectives. We don't feel the lack of a large home or a new car or a summer cottage or many of the other things that I would have acquired if I had stuck at one job since I was in my early 20s."

He said his work with people who are dying reminds him daily of the "transitional nature of life." And he went on to speak of his belief that "life is a process" and to say that "personal growth is more important to me than the achievements associated with my career." He said that in his early 30s he managed to discard the notion that he should fulfill his father's expectations, "which contributed to my acceptance of the idea that I don't need to control the future."

Derek sees his job as being closely intertwined with his real work—the things that matter deeply to him. But, he said, "there are things I do outside my job—singing, for example. I enjoy singing; I sing in a church choir and I take singing lessons. But I don't want it to be a burden to me. I do it as an amateur, as one who loves doing it."

But the thing that came through most conspicuously in talking with Derek is that he is a seeker—a sojourner, in fact. At one point he said, "What I'm doing is who I am. It allows me to be the person I want to be." But he also talked about having a "question about me and who I am. I have a question mark about who I am and why I am...what I am...why I believe and do the things I do. The process [of psychoanalysis] interests me very much, and I might take time out of my life and money to do that one day, to take a look at myself through analysis."

In his professional life, too, Derek is a mixture of confidence and humility. On the one hand, he talked about having high standards as a doctor—standards which make failure in that arena highly unlikely. But part of his professionalism is that, "I'm prepared to consult if I don't know what to do. If I don't know what to do in a case, I'm quite willing to go and ask someone else." Sometimes, he continued, "I recognize I'm not doing something the way it should be done. When I reach that point, I am aware of saying, `No that's not good enough. I've got to go back in the room and do this, or I've got to phone up a patient, or phone up a colleague, or whatever, but do something different and get enough information or enough of a consensus to do what I think is correct."

Derek is not a pious man, but he does take the spiritual dimension of his life seriously. "I try to pray each day. I'm not very successful in finding the time to meditate, except that I try to do that continuously throughout the day." His prayers, he said, have to do with acknowledging a power greater than himself and wanting to be "a funnel for that power." And he admitted that "coming to terms with the fact that life is not in my control" has been part of his spiritual development—and spiritual struggle.

He also talked about making choices without knowing the outcome. Looking over his career path to date, which has taken him from his native England to the Middle East, to Australia, back to England to study medicine, and then to Canada, he remarked, "what strikes me more than anything is how little information I had when I made the choices I did, and how I could not possibly have predicted the outcome of those choices. Many of them did not work out to be everything that I wanted. But they were fantastic; I enjoyed them. There were frustrating aspects, but I don't regret any of them. They were tremendous experiences. I learned something from each, and I gained something—maybe some spiritual maturity, which has made me believe that the choices are not that important but that what matters is the framework in which I exercise choice. That goes along with the concept of not needing to know the outcome." For him, that viewpoint is an integral part of "faith in a spiritual force, more powerful, more responsible and more in tune with what is right than I am."

Derek summed up at least part of his thinking by talking about planting a tree. "If I plant a tree, it's my choice to put that tree in the ground, but I do not choose how the tree will grow. I leave it up to the tree. I see myself as a custodian. I see myself as the planter, and the one who adds the fertilizer, and so forth. But not the one responsible for the outcome. If I create the right environment, then the outcome will look after itself. And I see myself as custodian of my own life, not the owner of it, not the director of it. I don't measure myself by its outcome."

Larry is another sojourner you have not previously met. Another photographer—and, in this case, a former public school teacher—Larry saw the salary he had as a teacher as "a means to an end. I started collecting art and after awhile the teaching, while I enjoyed it, became secondary. I looked forward to my weekends when I would be able to visit the art galleries. I took a great interest in photography, which came into the forefront in my life after about twenty years of teaching."

For Larry, the stresses of teaching mounted steadily and he found himself thinking, "maybe life's trying to tell me that this is not what I should be doing." Like Judith, however, he persevered, while at the same time determining that "I would do my teaching job as well as I could, but focus my priorities on my own private life."

For many people, that solution is a practical and workable one. They do their job to make a living, but find their primary satisfaction elsewhere. For Larry, however, even that kind of creative compromise eventually became intolerable: "I realized that life had been trying to tell me something and that for twenty-two years I had not been listening."

In talking about the choice he made, however, Larry also reflected on his lengthy tenure as a teacher and how he sees it. For quite awhile, he said, "I was enjoying what I was doing—especially working with the kids. The money was helpful because I was able to buy photography equipment and photos and art. There were rough points but I was able to get over them. It's just that the point finally came when it was time to get on to other things."

And so, in the middle of a recession, Larry resigned a job which paid a very healthy salary. Many people thought he was crazy. "But they didn't seem to realize that the money was not meaning anything to me anymore. I just felt that there was something in me that was missing. I felt empty inside."

At the time of my interview with Larry, he was less than a year into his life as a self-employed photographer. He was almost fifty, living with his parents while working to establish himself, knowing that it will almost certainly take at least two or three years to do so. It is the kind of decision not everyone would want to make. But Larry was confident it was the right one for him.

He acknowledged, however, that he may not work as a freelance photographer for the rest of his life. What is important is that he determined, in his words, "not to continue coasting along." He chose to be aware of his needs and to engage with his circumstances in light of those needs. That kind of consciousness, that kind of engagement, can take many forms. For Larry it meant a sharp break.

Larry talked of his identity as "a spark of creativity that is igniting into a flame that will spread out. That's how I define myself right now. I have more consciousness right now of my inner self, of who I really am, of what I can do than I've ever had before. It's taken me forty-nine years to come to that kind of awareness, but that's okay."

Finally, I want to introduce you to a man I'll call Garth, who is another sojourner I interviewed in the course of doing this book. Garth's sojourner "credentials" include being a sixth grade dropout, a survivor of childhood abuse in an orphanage, and a man who at one time had six assault charges brought against him—three of them involving police constables. His credentials also include being a recovered alcoholic who has been out of work numerous times and has held jobs ranging from candy maker to chef to construction worker to steeplejack to bartender. ("I was my best customer," he says of the last job, speaking from the vantage point of many years of sobriety.) Over the past decade, Garth has upgraded his education, completing training as a heating and power engineer, and has been employed for some years as the operations and maintenance manager of several office buildings.

His approach to his job—and to his life—is instructive. A few years ago, for example, he had a chance to attain a more senior position in his field. He took the job on a trial basis, but then returned to his old one. Such a decision would be unthinkable for many people. And I'm not suggesting that Garth made it without thoughtful deliberation; quite the contrary.

Having known him for awhile, however, I am not surprised by his choice. For his odyssey has left him with an unusual degree of centeredness. He has a pretty good sense of what is important to him and what isn't. "I didn't like the job," he told me, "because there was too much paperwork. It didn't suit me. I prefer working with a large cross section of people rather than looking after the budgets of a select few."

Part of what Garth likes about his job is the creativity it allows. "I can make changes at my level. I can get new ideas and opinions from people and put them into the works." And, he added, "I just have a good strong feeling inside that I am comfortable and good at my job." Finally, he explained, "I love to learn, I thoroughly enjoy that and the job is teaching me that. I don't know the job inside out. The job I've got, you're forever learning."

In addition to his regular responsibilities, Garth works with students training to be power engineers. Recently that included one with a major disability. "That was really hard. But that student taught me about patience—which I was starting to lose. When I was going through my studies I had patience and time and I wasn't in competition. But then I started to feel I was in competition with other people at work. The students helped to level me out. When I was competing with some other building managers, trying to do better than them, I felt something was lacking. When I was working with students, I was only in competition with myself. When I started to be in competition just with myself, everything improved."

He spoke with fondness and gratitude of being able to share time and responsibilities with his wife and of the importance of his children and grandchildren. But he also added, "I find I have to have one or two nights or a day or so by myself every week. I have to have that time by myself. It gives me time to think about everything on a 'no big deal' scale. For me to go for a walk with my dogs or to sit on a stump and just enjoy the sun and the beautiful blue sky, to cut a few cords of wood, that's great. I don't have to explain to anybody why I'm doing it, and lots of times I don't have any explanation. I'm just doing it because it feels comfortable."

It is apparent from talking with Garth that he values his job work identity. But it is also clear that there are other values in his life, and that some struggle has been involved in his discovery of them. Let me share with you something he said about one of his priorities:

"If I have one main goal in my life, it is to be more loving. Because there was a time in my life when I was not loving at all. Having gone from group home to group home to group home, having been molested as a child, I was not very loving at all—especially toward myself. Mainly I never learned how to love myself. I thought I was just not much. Today I know how to love myself a little but I need to learn to love myself even more. I can't be too hard on myself. I have to learn how to turn around and be more forgiving of my own mistakes."

The kind of love of self that Garth is talking about is not narcissistic. It is not love of one's image, of one's status, of one's place in the world. It is, rather, the kind of self-love which goes hand in hand with forgiveness, with self-discovery, with self-acceptance. It is love which embraces all of the paradoxes and contradictions that are part of being human, which recognizes that we are all mixtures of good and bad, success and failure, hope and discouragement, generosity and selfishness, faith and doubt, fear and courage.

To be obsessed with one part of ourselves—for example, with the job work self, with the place we occupy in the pecking order of things—is to close ourselves off from the kind of love that Garth described. But to see ourselves as sojourners—as those who attend responsibly and creatively to the present, to the place in which we currently find ourselves—is to become open to a sense of self that continues to unfold and to grow.

It is not that we should let go of one fixed identity in order to lay claim to another fixed one—although we never completely escape that tendency. The object is to move toward the kind of identity and awareness that allows for affirmation which goes beyond knowledge. Philosopher and author Sam Keen, whom I have quoted before, puts it poignantly when he says "Loving myself, I respect the mystery that I am. I open myself to *be* more than I can ever *know*."*

That kind of openness characterized the people I interviewed. In many ways they are ordinary people. Yet they are also extraordinary—not so much in their outer circumstances as in the quality of their inner lives. Their success lies not in the realm of standard accomplishments, but rather in the domain of atypical attitudes. They are less concerned with destination and arrival time, more open to the wonders of their journey.

But journeys do have their stopping places. And we are nearing the one that comes at the end of our exploration here. And so it is, in the next and final chapter, that I want to try to bring together a few things which are consistent with the stories we have read, the issues we have discussed, and the sojourner stance. They may prove to be of benefit as we continue along the way.

Chapter Eight

REMINDERS FOR THE JOURNEY

At the outset of this book I said that there are no simple answers to the issues we have been exploring here—issues having to do with selfhood, job work, and work beyond the job. Let me come back now to reaffirm that stance.

To be sure, we have listened to the stories of some people who have struggled creatively with those issues. And I hope that their stories will stimulate your imagination as you consider the challenges before you. But it should be understood that the stories are records of individual responses to individual circumstances. It would be a mistake to view any of them as recommending a particular course of action for yourself or others.

At the same time, I have discussed some principles and guidelines which can be useful to almost anyone in his or her journey of self-discovery, which can help persons move beyond the self-as-job syndrome. Knowing that they have been woven in various ways throughout the fabric of this book, I also know that it is sometimes hard to keep track of them.

I have therefore tried to pull together the main points of the book in the form of reminders—literally, *re-minders.* For they are approaches to living and working which can be easily lost or forgotten if they are not continually reaffirmed. I hope they will help you re-understand yourself and your potential more fully. They are intended to help you keep in mind a perspective which can contribute to healing and to courage, to hope and to love, to self-esteem and personal renewal.

Reminder Number 1: *Know and honor yourself and your story.* Remember that who you are is to be found not so much in your labels as in your story. To know yourself in depth is to know your journey. It is to know where you have been—in terms of job work, yes, but also in terms of friendships, relationships, struggles, cares, concerns, high points and low ones, in terms of stretches of straight, broad highway and sections of less traveled roads. Knowing yourself is not so much a matter of citing your resume as it is of paying attention to the myths that inform your choices—those that are working well and those that need to be discarded.

To know ourselves is to be clear about those things—which includes being clear about the compromises we may have to make in the course of making a living. Such compromises are all but unavoidable. But the better we know ourselves, the better we will be able to decide which ones are acceptable and which are not. It is difficult if not impossible to feel good about ourselves if we repeatedly do things which are counter to our values.

Implicit in what I am saying here is the importance of finding and claiming the neglected parts of ourselves—both the positive and the negative ones. That approach to selfhood is infinitely rewarding and empowering, but it is not easy. For identity and self-esteem come through self-knowledge, and self-knowledge in depth comes through struggle at least as much as through achievement. As we move beyond a self-as-job identity, therefore, it is important that we be kind to ourselves, that we give ourselves credit for our achievements and victories.

You will know by now that I do not recommend denying the "down" times of life. But at this point, as we affirm the value of knowing ourselves, I want to encourage you to think back over your life and remember things that have helped you to feel good about yourself. They do not have to be big things. They do not have to have had any commercial value. The only criterion is that they contributed to your positive regard of yourself. Take time to remember some of those moments, some of those occasions. They are part of who you are—and a part that should not be neglected. They are rightfully yours; you have every right to claim them.

The object of self-knowledge is to learn to accept yourself, value yourself, forgive yourself, love yourself, give creatively of yourself. And implicit in that objective is the importance of caring for yourself, of taking care of your whole person.

This includes taking care of yourself physically—eating for good nutrition, getting enough sleep, avoiding substances that are harmful to your physical well-being, and taking time for exercise. You do yourself a disservice when you neglect your body. It can often lead the way in strengthening both your mind and your spirit.

You can also nourish your inner life by taking time for solitude and, if you are so inclined, for prayer and meditation. Many people find the latter practices useful—and not only those who think of themselves as religious. And the creative gifts of others, which come to us in the form of music, art, and written and spoken words, are at-hand resources which can contribute immeasurably to emotional and spiritual well-being.

In addition, there are two other resources which can be of special value in knowing and valuing yourself. One is a sense of humor and the other is an attitude of gratitude. Both, I know, may at first seem strange in the context of a book whose focus is in large part on job work crises.

But a sense of humor is far from being incompatible with crisis. In fact, I believe it was Mark Twain who once said that the basis of all humor is sorrow, and most of us probably know the truth of that insight. For we may well remember times when we laughed to keep from crying—and, indeed, when we laughed and cried at the same time.

(I trust it is obvious that I am not talking here about humor that is hurtful and disparaging—of which there is far too much. Rather, I am talking about humor that includes the ability to laugh at ourselves. I am talking about humor which, with or without tears, recharges our souls and affirms our humanity.)

Likewise, it may seem that urging an attitude of gratitude is out of place here. But I suggest otherwise. For a true sense of identity comes with struggle, but it leads to a blend of confidence and humility, to awareness of the fact that we have been gifted. Our giftedness may not be as conspicuous as we would like. But it is in us.

We almost always have to peel through layers of shame and self-doubt to come to that awareness. Moreover, it is part of a strange truth which begins with the realization that we cannot be all that we feel we have to be. In accepting that reality, however, we open the way to being more than we thought possible.

To make that discovery is to come to an experience of grace and self-forgiveness. And that experience, however fleeting it is, can open us to a perspective, which, paradoxically, can find room from time to time for thanksgiving even in the midst of struggle.

Reminder Number 2: *Stay on the path of creative response.* Remember that it is neither our labels nor our circumstances that define who we are. Rather, it is how we respond to what happens to us. And we have the option of responding creatively. Which is to say that we have the option of drawing upon a resource that is at the center of all of life and that can be healing and strengthening in the here and now.

One way to cultivate our creativity is by staying curious, by accepting that we don't know how things are going to turn out. To take that stance does not rule out having dreams and goals. It does not deny the importance of throwing ourselves wholeheartedly into our efforts and ventures. Nor does it negate the fact that realizing our dreams and goals—large or small—can be beneficial to how we feel about ourselves.

But within the process of realizing our hopes and dreams should be a very important awareness—namely that trying too hard to force an end result can be unproductive. We can try so hard to "win" that we lose. To approach dreams and goals with openness, however, is to allow for the fact that they change. It is to *celebrate* the fact that they change. It is to allow for spontaneity and the unexpected, for the possibility that what we discover on the way to getting the things we think we want may turn out to be more valuable and precious than actually obtaining those things.

It is to understand that who we are—and how we feel about ourselves—is to be found in the process of living rather than in the realization of any particular outcome. It is to approach times of challenge in a spirit of "don't know"—which, as psychologist and spiritual teacher Joan Borysenko reminds us, "allows for stillness, and stillness for wisdom."*

A friend of mine, when asked a question having to do with how something or the other is likely to develop, frequently uses the expression, "it has not yet been revealed." To adopt the creative stance, the sojourner stance, is to be open to the unexpected, to that which is yet to be revealed.

Staying on the path of creative response is to live in a spirit of perpetual surrender—to let go of undue emotional attachment to the outcome of our efforts. To view life in that kind of framework does not eliminate the need to be responsible. Nor does it guarantee any particular kind of outcome.

Rather, that perspective springs from an approach to living in which faith, hope, and trust are intertwined. It is an approach that is consistent with the well known Serenity Prayer, which asks for serenity to accept the things that cannot be changed, courage to change the things that can, and wisdom to know the difference.

But it would be a mistake to think that creative living means passive living. For it requires courage. It requires that we engage with life, that we dialogue with it, that we take risks, that we imaginatively bring to life objects and options which otherwise would not come alive. Creativity involves vision and receptivity and "Aha!" moments. But it also involves action.

One way we can take action—and encourage our creativity—is by taking time to be creative. We can take time, that is, for creative self-expression. One of the unfortunate things about most job work is that it allows little opportunity for expressing ourselves and the values that matter most to us. To be sure, there are exceptions. If you have job work which falls into that category, count yourself indeed fortunate.

But remember that there are options for self-expression beyond the job work pale. I encourage you to find those that are meaningful and energizing to you. Draw, paint, sketch, write poetry, play music, drum, carve, make soup, bake bread, grow flowers, keep a journal—any of these avenues and countless others are invaluable means of discovering and affirming our sense of self. What is important is neither the particular channel nor the end result. What is important is that we express ourselves creatively.

Reminder Number 3: *It's permissible to take atypical paths.* You don't have to be overly concerned about the way things are "supposed to be." I am thinking in particular of the fact that in our culture, job work movement is always supposed to be "upward" if it is to be considered positive and that success is supposed to be measured in terms of tangible achievements.

But those notions can lead us astray, for they fly in the face of deeper truths. One of them is that the valleys of life are a part of real growth as surely as the mountaintops are. Another is that meaning and true success are to be found within a person rather than in external accomplishments. And a third is that our woundedness can contribute to our strength.

I am not suggesting that we should seek failure. But at times we may need to review our perspective. Willingness to do so was reflected in the stories of the people I interviewed. As you know by now, a number of them have had career paths with a downward curve—at least with respect to material success and security. But even when that pattern has been the operative one, they have "progressed." For they have been able to re-vision who they are and what is important to them.

Their stories can also remind us that we do have options and choices. They may not be the choices we would like. But they are invariably there—choices which lead away from despair, which enable us to say "yes" to life, even if hesitantly. At the very least, we can choose the attitude, the stance, that we take toward living and working. And that choice in itself can make a considerable difference in how we view our lives.

Reminder Number 4: *Attend to the present.* To accept that we don't know how things are going to turn out does not mean that we are to sit back and be indifferent. It is a receptive stance, to be sure, but it is not a passive one. It involves attending to the present, not to the future or to the past. It means doing what needs to be done next—making the phone call, writing the letter, sending the resume, mowing the yard, or calling on a friend.

Maybe the thing that needs attending to is your own quiet time, your own time to do nothing. Or it may be that you need to take time to play, to be spontaneous, to do something just for the fun of it. Remember that our real work includes all of those things. Remember that attending to the present means doing our best to savor and enjoy what is good in it.

Implicit in this reminder is the notion of mindfulness—of being fully present in whatever it is you are doing. Most of the time we waste energy by being unfocused, unconcentrated. We do one thing while thinking about another. There is great satisfaction to be found, however, in concentrating on whatever it is that is occupying our time—whether it is folding towels, studying the want ads, throwing a Frisbee, or gazing at a sunset or a blade of grass. Our inner sense of self is strengthened by that kind of focusing. It is a way of affirming our being now—not at some other point in time.

Reminder Number 5: *Recognize and claim your ability to change the focus of your attention.* Most of the time our attention is focused primarily on the material, the commercial, the external, the practical. All of these are important areas of life. But they are not the only ones. And we have the freedom and the power to pay attention to the others—to relationships, to creativity, to play, to mastery of a skill that may or may not have commercial value, to personal growth, to concern for others and for social justice.

To shift our focus of attention away from job work and toward other matters can help to strengthen our self-esteem and sense of identity. We cannot ignore completely the rules of the game called job work. But we do not have to limit ourselves to that game.

Reminder Number 6: *Don't try to go it alone.* One of the values emphasized by many of the people I talked with had to do with community—with the importance of putting individualism in perspective. We do not know ourselves in isolation. We do not find strength for the journey in isolation.

At times of stress, unfortunately, we are often tempted to withdraw from friends and family, from our relationships with the people most significant in our lives. To do so, however, is to shortchange ourselves. We need to pay attention to those relationships and to nourish them as much as possible.

It is true that we alone can choose wellness and well-being. But alone we cannot know their reality as fully as possible. Whether it be family, friends, a support group, a therapist, or all of the above, it is important to seek out supportive individuals and frameworks as we journey toward realizing our potential.

Reminder Number 7: *Get outside yourself.* Be open to opportunities for responding to the needs of others, for making a difference. As I have said many times, one of the values of job work is that it is a readily available, culturally approved means of making a difference. But there are others. And no one has to look far to see the needs of others—whether for a friend, for a big brother or sister, for help with any one of hundreds of worthy causes. By using our imaginations to the fullest, we can become better able to respond effectively to those needs. And in the process we can learn to see ourselves and our potential in a new light.

I am not suggesting that we neglect our own needs and priorities. But the truth is that part of finding ourselves has to do with giving of ourselves. And the fact is that the needs of our communities—and, for that matter, our planet—are crying out for attention.

Let me urge, therefore, that you take time to respond to needs around you, that you take time to discover for yourself that purpose and productivity in life do not have to depend on a paycheck. Acting on that truth can be empowering; it can contribute immensely to your sense of identity and your self-esteem. And it can make the world a better place in which to live.

Reminder Number 8: *Develop a perspective which embraces the paradoxes of life.* Don't get stuck in the limitations of either/or thinking. Accept and draw strength from the fact that life in depth is a both/and affair. Crises may be painful, but they invariably have within them the seeds of opportunity and renewal. That truth was seen repeatedly in the stories of the people we met in the course of this book.

Paradox runs throughout life. One example, mentioned earlier, is that we desire both change and permanence. And there are other examples: We at once are unlike any other human being, yet we are not islands unto ourselves. We grow and move on by letting go, by repeatedly experiencing "necessary losses." We can find strength by claiming our woundedness and vulnerability.

Yet another paradox, related to the last one, is that our strengths and weaknesses are not opposites but are, instead, almost invariably interrelated. Our successes and our failures sometimes have common roots. That which we see as "bad" in ourselves is often that which is "good" carried to extremes.

For example, trust is a positive quality. Without discernment, however, it can become naiveté, which is not. Concern for quality can easily become perfectionism. Tolerance can turn to indifference. The dark side of a passion for life is addiction. And the list could go on.

And, finally, we need to remember that our neglected parts often contain that which is most vital and real about us. We saw examples of that paradox in Norman, who by embracing the creativity and sensitivity he had neglected has gotten a new lease on life, and in Frank, who gained a stronger sense of selfhood by embracing his "oddballness" in the course of a dream.

In both cases we saw illustrated the truth that we add to our strength and our identity not by a process of denial and exclusion but rather by one of inclusion, of acceptance, of drawing upon all parts of who we are creatively and responsibly.

Reminder Number 9: *Be a lifelong learner.* I am not only talking about reading books and taking courses—though I believe strongly in the value of both. What I also have in mind, however, is learning from experience—being open to new insights about yourself and your surroundings.

If there was one single trait that was characteristic of all of the people I interviewed, it was that here were people who were curious, who were open to learning from their experience. However challenging the task may have been, they were making new discoveries in the course of their journeys. They were people whose sense of identity was continuing to grow and to deepen. For them, life is something that continues to unfold. Rather than measuring it against rigid concepts and expectations, they interact with it and learn from it.

It is a common belief that human beings develop according to a fixed sequence, especially with respect to learning. And there is no question that people can—and often do—"shut down" once they have reached a certain stage. But the invitation is always there for all of us to make new discoveries, to respond creatively to what is being revealed, and to be curious about what will be revealed next.

Reminder Number 10: *Remember that job work is only a part of who you are—that your real work goes beyond your job work.* Job work is what we do for pay. Our real work, which may or may not include job work, has to do with participating as fully and creatively and constructively as possible in the life we are given.

Job work exists in well-defined places and times and can be easily interrupted. Real work, while it can be neglected, can be done under any circumstances. It can be done while we are waiting for job work to begin or to continue.

Job work is about "bottom line" productivity. Real work involves productivity which comes out of what Jungian therapist Frances Wickes termed "the workshop of the soul whose windows open upon inner and outer worlds."* Job work is about making a living. Real work is about making a life.

To suggest that our real work has to do with full participation in life does not mean trying to do everything. What it does mean, I suggest, is not neglecting major parts of life and our potential. To put all of our attention on job work is to do just that. It is to shortchange ourselves. For most job work today ignores significant parts of human experience.

Most job work, for example, does not place much of a premium on self-expression—competency, yes, but not creativity. Most job work does not involve crafting anything. The emphasis is on selling, reshuffling, and rearranging. Most job work allows little if any opportunity for the expression of feelings. It assuredly does not allow for falling down, for failure—which, with all its pain, is an integral and potentially rich part of human life. Nor does job work allow much opportunity for play or for community, office picnics and parties notwithstanding. And, finally, most job work tends to squeeze out time for deep and lasting relationships.

Job work is important; it can contribute enormously to self-esteem and a sense of identity, especially if it provides a fair wage and a sense of accomplishment. I wish you every success in finding that kind of employment.

But other things can provide meaning and satisfaction too. And we need to find and claim for ourselves those alternatives that are healthy, sustainable, and perhaps even more satisfying. We need to search for creative options which will allow job work to be the servant of our real work and not the other way around.

The question *"What do you do?"* will continue to be asked. And, for many people, it will continue to be understood in a limited way—as *"What do you do for a living?" "What is your paid occupation?" "What is your assigned social role?"*

For those who so choose, however, it can be understood in a different way—as *"What do you do to make a life?" "What do you do to develop your potential?" "What do you do to deepen your relationships with those who are significant in your life?" "What do you do for the good of your community, your planet?" "What do you do with your time—and for what purpose?" "What do you do to awaken and nourish your soul and your spirit?" "What do you do to bring to life your unique giftedness?" "What do you do to share your giftedness with others?"*

The object in raising those questions, and in attempting to reinterpret one of the most common questions of our culture, is to try to help you see that there is a choice in how you respond—not only to the question *"What do you do?"* but to the challenges and opportunities that are present in your daily living. The object is to help you discover that you do not have to think of the question in the constricted way in which it is usually understood.

For you do not have to be limited to a one-dimensional, job-work view of who you are. Your value as a human being is not limited to anyone's financial bottom line. Your self-esteem can come more from within you than from the external factors in your life. You can affirm that truth—and yourself—in the ways we have discussed. And you can do so now, in the present.

To reinterpret the question is, therefore, to emphasize that you truly are more than your job.

FOOTNOTES

Chapter One

Page 3 ...who will I say that I am when I go to a party? Judith Viorst, *Necessary Losses* (New York: Ballantine Books, 1987), pp. 310-311.

Page 5 ...failure at that type of work was a sign of damnation, Eric Fromm, *Escape From Freedom* (New York: Avon Books, 1965), p. 112.

Page 5 ...not so much by external pressure but by an internal compulsion, Fromm, *Escape From Freedom,* p. 113.

Page 5 ...work as personal fulfillment had come to be subordinated to work as productivity, Theodore Roszak, *Person/Planet—The Creative Disintegration of Industrial Society* (Garden City, New York: Anchor Press/Doubleday, 1978), p. 213.

Page 6 ...ceased to have a natural, established place in the economic and social order, Fromm, *Escape From Freedom,* p. 77.

Page 6 ...namely that personality is a commodity, Fromm, *Escape From Freedom,* p. 140.

Page 7 ...a means of maintaining a link between the spiritual and the material in human life, Jacob Needleman, *Money and the Meaning of Life* (New York: Doubleday, 1991), p. 114.

Page 8 ...only those things that money can buy, Needleman, *Money and the Meaning of Life,* p. 112.

Page 14 ...the dictate that success can cover up any flaw, Roger Gould, M.D., *Transformations* (New York: Simon & Schuster/Touchstone, 1978), p. 230.

Page 14 ...letting go of them can indeed feel like death, Gerald May, M.D., *Addiction and Grace.* (San Francisco: Harper & Row, 1988), p. 100

Page 15 ...a kind of container within our personality, Carol Pearson, *Awakening the Heroes Within* (San Francisco: Harper San Francisco, 1991), p. 28.

Chapter Two

Page 32 ...committed what he called egocide, J. Baldwin, "The Dymaxion" *Harrowsmith* Magazine (Number One Hundred, Vol. XVI:4, November-December, 1991), p. 69.

Page 35 ...point the way toward who one may become, Helen Merrell Lynd, *On Shame and the Search for Identity* (New York: Harcourt, Brace and World, 1958), p. 20.

Page 35 ...may be the point of opportunity for his or her next area of development, Robert Johnson, *Owning Your Own Shadow* (San Francisco: Harper San Francisco, 1991), p. 92.

Page 41 ...having to do with depth, value, relatedness, heart, and personal substance, Thomas Moore, *Care of the Soul—A Guide for Cultivating Depth and Sacredness in Everyday Life.* (New York: HarperCollins Publishers, 1992), p. 5.

Page 43 ...by appreciating failure with imagination, we reconnect it to success, Moore, *Care of the Soul,* pp. 196-197.

Page 43 ...it is when the unstoppable bullet hits the impenetrable wall that we have our deepest experiences, Johnson, *Owning Your Own Shadow,* p. 92.

Page 44 ...by the raw materials of our own experience—our own "catastrophe"–whatever it may be, Jon Kabat-Zinn, *Full Catastrophe Living* (New York: Delacorte Press, 1990), p. 11.

Page 45 ...failure to fall apart may be as unhealthy as the failure to find a new way to grow following a crisis, Frederich Flach, M.D., *Resilience—Discovering a New Strength at Times of Stress* (New York: Fawcett Columbine, 1988), pp. 38, 49.

Chapter Three

Page 49 ...which in fact lie among dusty memories, Carl Jung, "The Stages of Life," first published in 1933. In *The Portable Jung,* edited, with an introduction, by Joseph Campbell, translated by R.F.C. Hull (New York: Penguin Books, 1976), p. 12.

Page 51 ...the models by which human beings code and organize their perceptions, feelings, thoughts, and actions, Stanley Krippner, *Personal Mythology—The Psychology of Your Evolving Self* (Los Angeles: Jeremy P. Tarcher, Inc., 1988), p. 2.

Page 61 ...three phases: separation, initiation, and return, Joseph Campbell, *The Hero with a Thousand Faces,* Second Edition (Princeton: Princeton University Press, 1968), p. 30.

Page 61 ...becoming more fully alive and more effective in the world, Pearson, *Awakening the Heroes Within,* p. 1.

Page 62 ...those parts of ourselves that we do not want to acknowledge, Connie Zweig and Jeremiah Abrams, eds., *Meeting the Shadow—The Hidden Power of the Dark Side of Human Nature* (Los Angeles: Jeremy P. Tarcher, Inc., 1991), pp. 3-4.

Page 63 ...our shadow is also revealed when we project the best of ourselves onto others, Johnson, *Owning Your Own Shadow*, p. 42.

Page 64 ...our fate can truly be altered if we have the courage to embrace the opposites, Johnson, *Owning Your Own Shadow*, p. 55.

Page 72 ...more like the raw material awaiting a builder, William Bridges, *Transitions* (Reading, Massachusetts: Addison-Wesley Publishing Co., 1980), p. 123.

Page 79 ...was a kind of metaphor for those committed to success and all its trappings, Jean Shinoda Bolen, *Gods in Everyman—A New Psychology of Men's Lives and Loves* (New York: Harper & Row/Perennial Library, 1990), p. 281.

Page 80 ...to welcome all the diversity of experience into consciousness, Sam Keen, *The Passionate Life: Stages of Loving.* (San Francisco: Harper & Row, 1983), p. 164.

Chapter Four

Page 82 ...self-actualizing creativity, Abraham Maslow, *Toward a Psychology of Being,* Second Edition (New York: Van Nostrand Reinhold, 1968), p. 137.

Page 82 ...of all the creative arts the most difficult and the most distinguished, Frances Wickes, *The Inner World of Choice* (Boston: Sigo Press, 1988), p. 1.

Page 84 ...life is either a daring adventure or nothing, quoted in Richard J. Leider, *The Power of Purpose* (New York: Ballantine Books, 1985), p. 28.

Page 85 ...may in fact be the ones with the greatest artistic merit, Mihaly Csikszentmihalyi, *Flow—The Psychology of Optimal Experience* (New York: Harper Perennial, 1991), pp. 208 and 277; Michael Ray and Rochelle Myers, *Creativity in Business* (New York: Doubleday and Company, Inc., 1986), pp. 15-16.

Page 86 ...there have never been rites to keep winter from coming, Campbell, *The Hero With a Thousand Faces.* p. 384.

Page 87 ...a master key to creativity, Stephen Nachmanovitch, *Free Play—The Power of Improvisation in Life and the Arts* (Los Angeles, Jeremy P. Tarcher, Inc., 1990), p. 6.

Page 98 ...human beings can find meaning in three principal ways, Viktor Frankl, *The Will to Meaning* (New York: New American Library, 1969), p. 70.

Page 102 ...control is primarily a belief, Blair Justice, *Who Gets Sick* (Houston: Peak Press, 1987), p. 61.

Page 102 ...from an inner certainty or faith about one's place in life, Larry Dossey, *Meaning and Medicine* (New York: Bantam Books, 1991), pp. 67-68.

Page 104 ...to let go of any emotional attachment to the final outcome, Ray and Myers, *Creativity in Business*, p. 14.

Page 108 ...for art to appear, we have to disappear, Nachmanovitch, *Free Play*, p. 51.

Page 110 ...really serious problems of life are unsolvable, Carl Jung, "The Stages of Life," *The Portable Jung*, p. 11.

Chapter Five

Page 114 ...a deepseated part of the human makeup, R.D. Laing, *Self and Others* (New York: Pelican, 1971), p. 136.

Page 116 ...a wasteland of dry stones, Campbell, *Hero With a Thousand Faces*, p. 59.

Page 118 ...lifeline for survival, Julius Segal, *Winning Life's Toughest Battles—Roots of Human Resilience* (New York: Ballantine/Ivy Books, 1986), p. 12.

Page 118 ...if you want to survive a tragedy, you need a friend, Robert Veninga, *A Gift of Hope* (New York: Ballantine Books, 1985), p. 59.

Chapter Six

Page 139 ...providing the foundation for meeting other human needs, Maslow, *Toward a Psychology of Being*, Second Edition, pp. 44 ff.

Page 150 ...really about paying attention, Kabat-Zinn, *Full Catastrophe Living*, pp. 20-21.

Page 150 ...without knowing what it was or when we lost it, Lawrence LeShan, *How to Meditate—A Guide to Self-Discovery* (New York: Bantam, 1975), p. 1.

Page 153 ...doing and being for its own pure joy, Nachmanovitch, *Free Play,* p. 43.

Page 153 ...the spark that makes life worth living, Rick Fields, with Peggy Taylor, Rex Weyler, and Rick Ingrasci, *Chop Wood, Carry Water—A Guide to Finding Spiritual Fulfillment in Everyday Life* (Los Angeles: Jeremy P. Tarcher, Inc., 1984), p. 143.

Page 154 ...the therapeutic value of laughter in his recovery, Norman Cousins, *The Anatomy of an Illness* (New York: Bantam Books, 1981), pp. 39 ff.

Page 155 ...and begin to see the patterns within the seeming chaos, Gabriele Rico, *Pain and Possibility—Writing Your Way Through Personal Crisis* (Los Angeles: Jeremy P. Tarcher, Inc., 1991), p. 7.

Page 156 ...expressing your feelings in writing may actually help in the job search process, James Pennebaker, quoted in "News and Trends" section, *Psychology Today,* (March/April, 1993), p. 14.

Page 157 ...so that we can continue living our narrative in a creative way, Joseph Gold, *Read for Your Life—Literature as a Life Support System* (Markham, Ontario: Fitzhenry & Whiteside, 1990), p. 4.

Page 157 ...a way for staying in shape, Csikszentmihalyi, *Flow,* p. 130.

Page 162 ...continuous adjustment to continuous change, Nachmanovitch, *Free Play,* pp. 48-49.

Chapter Seven

Page 166 ...life begins with loss, Viorst, *Necessary Losses,* p. 9.

Page 169 ...when we are lost and searching, stumbling and falling, Ernest Kurtz, *The Spirituality of Imperfection* (New York: Bantam, 1992), p. 134.

Page 181 ...I open myself to be more than I can ever know. Sam Keen, *The Passionate Life,* p. 164.

Chapter Eight

Page 187 ...which allows for stillness, and stillness for wisdom, Joan Borysenko, *Fire in the Soul* (New York: Warner Books, Inc., 1993), p. 155.

Page 193 ...whose windows open upon inner and outer worlds, Wickes, *The Inner World of Choice.,* p. 1.

ABOUT THE AUTHOR

Earl Harrison describes himself as a writer, a husband, a father, and a man who is still learning. Formerly a university professor, he has also worked as a private consultant/counselor in the fields of addiction and career and mid-life transitions. His recent credits include co-writing and co-producing the award-winning Canadian TV docudrama series *The 12 Steps: Recovering From Addictions.*